The Elephant in the Room

The Elephant in the Room

Silence and Denial in Everyday Life

Eviatar Zerubavel

OXFORD
UNIVERSITY PRESS
2006

OXFORD
UNIVERSITY PRESS

Oxford University Press, Inc., publishes works that
further Oxford University's objective of excellence
in research, scholarship, and education.

Oxford   New York
Auckland   Cape Town   Dar es Salaam   Hong Kong   Karachi
Kuala Lumpur   Madrid   Melbourne   Mexico City   Nairobi
New Delhi   Shanghai   Taipei   Toronto

With offices in
Argentina   Austria   Brazil   Chile   Czech Republic   France   Greece
Guatemala   Hungary   Italy   Japan   Poland   Portugal   Singapore
South Korea   Switzerland   Thailand   Turkey   Ukraine   Vietnam

Published by Oxford University Press, Inc.
198 Madison Avenue, New York, NY 10016
www.oup.com

Library of Congress Cataloging-in-Publication Data
Zerubavel, Eviatar.
The elephant in the room : silence and denial in everyday life /
Eviatar Zerubavel.
p. cm.
Includes bibliographical references.
ISBN-13: 978-0-19-518717-5
ISBN-10: 0-19-518717-2
1. Denial (Psychology)—Social aspects.
2. Avoidance (Psychology)—Social aspects.
3. Silence. 4. Secrecy. 5. Social psychology.
I. Title.
HM1041.Z47 2006
302.2—dc22   2005023273

1 3 5 7 9 8 6 4 2
Printed in the United States of America
on acid-free paper

To Noam,

whose courage to see, hear, and speak I admire

Contents

Preface

The seeds of this book date back to my childhood. Growing up in a home where every single room housed some unmentionable "elephant," I was always surrounded by "open secrets" that, although widely known, nevertheless remained unspoken. Similarly significant in this regard was the experience of growing up in the 1950s in Tel Aviv, where most of what remained from the pre-1948 non-Jewish past of some of its neighborhoods were their Arab names. Witnessing years later the tremendous pain suffered by individuals who try to resist collective efforts to quash "elephants" through forced silence further triggered my interest in the nuanced tension between what is personally experienced and what is publicly acknowledged.

Yet it was a particular experience I had as a director of a doctoral program that ultimately inspired me to write this book. In the spring of 1998 I found myself in a situation of having to deal with a most disturbing series of events that threatened the social and moral fabric of my department yet that, for an unusual combination of reasons involving both fear and shame, although widely known and insidiously pervasive, were nevertheless publicly ignored by many of my colleagues. Like the situation itself, I found their response to it personally distressing yet at the same time intellectually fascinating. Having written about the social aspects of the process of noticing, I became increasingly interested in the social aspects of the process of ignoring. I was also becoming increasingly aware of the highly problematic long-term impact of silence on individuals as well as on entire groups.

The following year I presented an early overview of my evolving ideas about the social organization of silence and denial at a national conference hosted by my department. My talk generated a lot of discussion, yet of the dozen or so of my colleagues who attended only two mentioned it to me later, which exemplified my argument about our general reluctance to openly talk about not talking. Three years later, in November 2002, I started to write this book.

In her memoir *After Silence: Rape and My Journey Back*, Nancy Raine describes how difficult it is to write about silence, since the very act of writing often evokes precisely the painful themes about which one is writing. And indeed, although this is the ninth book I have written, none of the others was so difficult for me to write. Spending entire days writing and rewriting sentences that were evidently far too evocative for me, I suddenly understood for the first time why the Hebrew words for silence and paralysis are actually derived from the same root. While writing about silence, therefore, talking with others can become a cherished necessity, and I am particularly grateful in this regard to Kathy Gerson, Debby Carr, Jenna Howard, Ruth Simpson, Ira Cohen, Allan Horwitz, Ethel Brooks, Miriam Bauer, Dan Ryan, Karen Cerulo, Ellen Idler, Carolyn Williams, and Suzanne Zatkowsky for helping me avoid becoming totally engulfed by the overwhelming, painful silence surrounding me.

Yael Zerubavel, Ruth Simpson, Debby Carr, Tom DeGloma, Dan Ryan, Chris Nippert-Eng, Kathy Gerson, Jenna Howard,

Arlie Hochschild, Lynn Chancer, Allan Horwitz, Samantha
Spitzer, Kari Norgaard, Johanna Foster, and Wayne Brekhus
were kind enough to read early drafts of the manuscript and
offer many helpful suggestions for improvement. I also ben-
efited tremendously from discussing my evolving ideas with
my children Noga and Noam Zerubavel as well as with Kristen
Purcell, Anat Helman, Kathryn Harrison, Carolyn Barber,
Viviana Zelizer, Robin Wagner-Pacifici, Jan Lewis, Doug
Mitchell, Frances Milliken, Ann Mische, and Zali Gurevitch. I
would also like to thank my editor, Tim Bartlett, for helping
me present those ideas in a way that would make them more
accessible to a wider audience, as well as the John Simon
Guggenheim Memorial Foundation, whose 2003 fellowship,
generously complemented by Rutgers University, allowed me
to take a year off during which I could fully dedicate myself to
writing it. Thanks are also due to Paula Cooper for a terrific job
of editing the manuscript.

Finally, a special thank-you to my wife, companion, and life-
long friend Yael Zerubavel, who was with me throughout this
long, arduous journey. Thank you for your nonsilent understanding and support.

East Brunswick, New Jersey
June 2005

We will have to repent in this generation not merely for the hateful words and actions of the bad people but for the appalling silence of the good people.

—Martin Luther King Jr.
"Letter From Birmingham Jail," April 16, 1963

The Elephant in the Room

chapter One

A Conspiracy of Silence

Although I know Aunt Lace knew about the rape—and, of course, she knew I knew my mother had told her—we never mentioned it. I never brought it up, nor did she.

—Nancy Raine, *After Silence*

Open Secrets

There is a famous fourteenth-century Castilian story about a Moorish king duped by three swindlers into believing that a dazzling new suit they are supposedly weaving for him is somehow invisible to any person of illegitimate birth. Embarrassed to admit he cannot see the glamorous fabric, a servant sent to inspect their work reports that good progress is being made. A second servant soon comes back and corroborates this account. The king then goes to see the fabric for himself. Fearing that if he were to admit he cannot actually see anything he might lose his legitimacy and consequently his kingdom, he proceeds to praise the invisible cloth lavishly. This then leads a constable, obviously concerned about his own reputation, also to extol it, which understandably makes the king even more embarrassed that he cannot see it.

When the delusion is further corroborated by yet another sycophant who dares not admit that he cannot really see anything, the king then proudly rides into town to display his imaginary suit, and although it is invisible to all, "everyone thought that his neighbors saw it, and that if they did not, and said so, they would be ruined and disgraced." Only one brave man finally tells the king that "either I am blind or you are naked" and soon "everyone was saying it, until the monarch and everyone else ceased to be afraid of knowing the truth."[1]

This delightful story was famously retold five centuries later by Hans Christian Andersen. Andersen basically kept it intact, making only a few minor changes such as linking the fabric's invisibility to the viewer's stupidity rather than illegitimacy and transforming Western literature's archetypal whistleblower from a self-consciously defiant African into a naive child. Like its original author, Don Juan Manuel, he was particularly fascinated by the fundamental tension it so effectively portrays between the private act of noticing and the public act of acknowledging: "'It is magnificent! Beautiful! Excellent!' All of their mouths agreed, though none of their eyes had seen anything."[2] It is this glaring incongruity between interiority and exteriority, perception and expression, that makes "The Emperor's New Clothes" such a captivating story.

The story highlights an intriguing social phenomenon commonly known as a conspiracy of silence, whereby a group of people tacitly agree to outwardly ignore something of which they are all personally aware, such as the sexual liaisons between masters and slaves in the antebellum South or the presence of functionally illiterate student athletes on many American campuses today.[3] Essentially revolving around common knowledge that is practically never discussed in public, undiscussables and unmentionables that are "generally known but cannot be spoken," such "open secrets" constitute "uncomfortable truths hidden in plain sight," to quote Paul Krugman.[4]

Such "silent witnessing" is distinctly characterized by each conspirator's awareness of the open secret as well as his reluctance to express it publicly.[5] It is this fundamental tension between knowledge and acknowledgement, personal awareness and public discourse, that makes "The Emperor's New Clothes" such an evocative commentary on social life.

See No Evil, Hear No Evil, Speak No Evil

To better understand how one can actually be aware and (at least publicly) unaware of something at the same time it is useful to invoke here the notion of "denial."[6] Extending this notion beyond the way it was originally conceived by Freud to denote a strictly intrapersonal phenomenon, however, I am specifically interested in the sociology rather than the psychology of denial.[7]

As we shall see, denial is a product of individual as well as collective efforts. In her memoir *The Kiss*, Kathryn Harrison tries to suppress her awareness of the increasingly sexualized nature of her relations with her father through "selective self-anesthesia." This leaves her "awake to certain things and dead to others," and the mechanisms of denial she employs are unmistakably psychological. Yet when her boyfriend, obviously threatened by what she tells him, collusively helps her forget it, we are actually witnessing a joint effort to essentially co-ignore it.[8] And while psychologists try to unravel the intrapersonal dynamics of blocking certain information from entering individuals' awareness, my goal here is to examine the interpersonal dynamics of keeping it from entering their public conversation. As evidenced by the way we often use numbness imagery to portray it, being in a state of denial usually involves a quasi-sensorial shutoff. As conventional metaphoric allusions to "blind spots" as well as images such as "looking the other way" or "turning a blind eye" seem to indicate, we tend to equate being out of sight with being out of mind. It is hardly surprising, then, that we often associate denial with blindness. (As an incest survivor describes her family's failure to acknowledge her plight, "everyone is blind in my father's house.")[9] In fact, upon realizing the extent of his own denial, Oedipus actually blinds himself. The image of "turning a deaf ear" as well as the way we sometimes cover our ears as if to block certain information from entering our awareness are also best understood in this context.

Yet the way we corporeally refrain from receiving information also mirrors the way we corporeally avoid transmitting it to others. As the image of "biting one's tongue" and the ritual of covering one's mouth after saying something one shouldn't both seem to indicate, the simplest way not to acknowledge something of which we are personally aware is to remain silent. Indeed, the most public form of denial is silence.

Conspiracies of silence presuppose mutual denial, whereby at least two people collaborate to jointly avoid acknowledging something. This is perfectly exemplified by the "don't ask, don't tell" United States military policy toward homosexuals. It takes at least two persons to "dance the familiar conspiracy tango—one not to tell, the other not to ask," to quote I. F. Stone.[10] Indeed, such "conspiracies" are often represented in the form of three monkeys who see no evil, hear no evil, and speak no evil.

The well-known image of this traditional Japanese simian trio[11] perfectly embodies the symbiotic relations between being blind, deaf, and mute. The fact that its members are always presented together seems to point to social systems such as families, organizations, and communities as the natural context for studying conspiracies of silence. Yet looking at the distinctly social structure of denial also underscores the way various features of social relations (such as the extent to which they are hierarchical) as well as social situations (such as the extent to which they are public) affect the likelihood of actually engaging in such conspiracies, as noted, for example, by Elizabeth Morrison and Frances Milliken: "Imagine an organization where the CEO has no clothes. The CEO's lack of clothes is apparent to all . . . Yet employees never mention this . . . Behind the safety of closed doors and in veiled whispers, they talk of their leader's lack of clothing . . . but only the foolish or naive dare to speak of it in public."[12] In short, as the quintessential public manifestation of denial, conspiracies of silence are clearly socially patterned.

Fear and Embarrassment

According to many psychologists, denial stems from our need to avoid pain. When awareness of something particularly distressful threatens our psychological well-being, we often activate inner floodgates that block the disturbing information from entering our consciousness. This point is sensitively portrayed in the film *Music Box*, in which a loving daughter tries somehow to "explain it away" when faced with growing evidence of the war atrocities committed by her father.

As a form of denial, silence certainly helps us avoid pain. The fact that something is considered "too terrible for words" indeed often makes it literally unspeakable. That explains the heavy silence that usually surrounds atrocities. "We don't talk about

them . . . because they're too horrific."[13] Many Holocaust survivors, for example, thus refrain from sharing their traumatic
experiences with their children to avoid the terrible pain they
evoke. Grandparents and half-siblings who died during those
"unmentionable years" thus often remain wrapped in a blanket
of silence.[14]

As some of those survivors refer to their horrific time in the
Nazi death camps as "the war,"[15] identifying such euphemisms
may help uncover conspiracies of silence by highlighting what
they consider unmentionable. Yet a careful examination of euphemisms also seems to show that trauma is only one of the
factors that produce silence. Indeed, most conspiracies of silence are generated by the two main reasons we actually use
euphemisms, namely fear and embarrassment.[16]

When facing a frightening situation, we often resort to denial.
In fact, early reports of Nazi massacres of Jews were dismissed
by many Jews in Europe as sheer lies.[17] As a result, frightening
information often becomes essentially undiscussable.[18] As so
chillingly exemplified by the numerous bystanders who silently
witnessed the blatant implementation of the "Final Solution,"
people who live in police states become increasingly reluctant
to publicly acknowledge the brutality that surrounds them by
discussing it with others.[19] Fear is also one of the main reasons
underlying the abundance of euphemisms used in reference to
the terminally ill ("when this is over") and the dead ("passed
away," "gone") as well as the ominous silence surrounding the
specter of a nuclear war.[20]

Sex, too, is often considered a somewhat threatening and
therefore unmentionable subject. A former seminarian describes
the prohibitive silence surrounding, for example, the sexual life
of Catholic clergy (not to mention the homoerotic form it often takes):

Seminary teaching on purity . . . warned, cajoled, threatened, satirized, but it did not describe. The thing itself was often left in the dark . . . The tense silence about sex was perhaps nowhere more noticeable than after dismissals. When someone was sent away for failing to demonstrate a vocation to celibacy, little or nothing was said. Seminarians just disappeared. The assigned place in choir closed up. The room or dorm bed was cleaned and someone else was moved into it . . . [Sex] was too awful or ugly or threatening to be spoken.[21]

Yet as illustrated by hushed-up instances of illegitimacy, teen pregnancy, or infidelity,[22] the silence surrounding sex also stems from shame, as did much of the silence originally surrounding the Holocaust. (Thus, for example, during the 1950s, German children usually avoided asking their fathers what they did during the war, while at school German history often "stopped at Bismarck.")[23]

Yet silence is also generated by the somewhat milder form of shame we call embarrassment,[24] as when a group of scholars are asked to evaluate a well-liked yet obviously unproductive colleague, when pastors discover incidents of domestic violence in their own parish, or when co-workers watch aging physicians lose their clinical touch.[25] Consider also hushed-up instances of suicide, mental illness, or alcohol abuse within families, as when a young child comes home "with his mother and younger brother to find his father passed out in the living room with furniture in disarray and dishes scattered all around him . . . [N]o one [says] a word while the mess [is] quietly cleaned up . . . Nothing [is] said the following morning either."[26] Equally illustrative in this regard are Israel's official silence about the destruction of Arab villages during its War of Independence and the scant attention paid by the American media to Irish-Americans' role in helping finance Irish terror in Britain or to the fact that the senior member of the United States Senate, Robert Byrd, is a former member of the Ku Klux Klan. Along similar lines, consider also Western intellectuals' silence about the horrors of Stalinism during the 1930s (or Arab intellectuals' silence about Iraq's brutal occupation of Kuwait in 1990, for that matter) as well as African leaders' obvious reluctance to publicly acknowledge President Robert Mugabe's dismal civil rights record in Zimbabwe.[27]

Needless to say, the distinction between conspiracies of silence that are generated by pain, fear, shame, and embarrassment is strictly analytical. After all, as we have seen, the silence surrounding the Holocaust, for example, has in fact been a product of both pain, fear, and shame. A combination of both fear and embarrassment likewise generates silence in situations where an incompetent fellow employee also happens to be the boss's son.

The Heavy Sound of Silence

As linguists and others studying human communication systems have repeatedly pointed out, silence is actually "part of [our] communicative system comparable with speech." A pronouncedly active performance, it entails "neither muteness nor mere absence of audible sound," as it "fills the pauses and cracks and crannies of our discourse."[28] Indeed, as Paul Simon suggests in his famous song, it actually has an unmistakable sound, and as our conventional images of "thick," "deafening," "heavy," or "resounding" silences seem to imply, it often speaks louder than words. After many years in which her daughter begged her to tell her about their relatives who were killed by the Nazis, one Holocaust survivor finally complied by sending her four virtually blank pages.[29]

Indeed, silence often involves an unspoken conversation. "What is she not saying?" wonders another Holocaust survivor's daughter about her mother.[30] And in the film *Waiting for the Messiah*, when asked by his son what they should do about their family's financial problems, a father replies, "Not tell Mother. That's all we can do."

In his short story "Silence," Leonid Andreyev specifically contrasts stillness, "the mere absence of noise," with silence, "which means that those who kept silent could . . . have spoken if they had pleased."[31] Being silent thus involves more than just absence of action, since the things about which we are silent are in fact actively avoided. The careful absence of explicit race labels in current American liberal discourse, for example, is indeed the product of a deliberate effort to suppress our awareness of race.[32] Ironically, such deliberate avoidance may actually produce the opposite result. (As Bing Crosby wryly notes toward the end of the film *The Country Girl* upon suddenly realizing how close his wife and best friend have actually become, "there is only one thing more obvious than two people looking longingly at each other and it's two people avoiding it.")

Like silence, denial involves active avoidance. Rather than simply failing to notice something, it entails a deliberate effort to refrain from noticing it.[33] Furthermore, it usually involves refusing to acknowledge the presence of things that actually beg for attention, thereby reminding us that conspiracies of silence revolve not around those largely unnoticeable matters we simply overlook but, on the contrary, around those highly conspicuous matters we deliberately try to avoid.[34]

That explains the increasingly common use of an elephant to metaphorically represent the object of such conspiracies, as so poignantly depicted in the following satirical portrait of collective denial from the 2000 American presidential campaign:

> You wouldn't know it from the media coverage, but there was an elephant sucking up the oxygen in the cozy room where aspiring vice-presidents Dick Cheney and Joe Lieberman conducted their recent soporific, kid-gloved debate . . . [T]he elephant was none other than the specter of Mary Cheney, Dick's openly, publicly, and lately, not only morally, but physically invisible, lesbian daughter. The spectral elephant sat there between the two candidates, frantically curling and uncurling her massive trunk until the big question of the night came along. "Senator, sexual orientation." The elephant trumpeted. But the two candidates, their courtly chat moderator, CNN's Bernard Shaw, and the national media, pretended she wasn't there.[35]

Equally evocative in this regard is the aptly titled handbook for helping children of alcoholics, *An Elephant in the Living Room*, which portrays alcohol abuse as a big elephant whose ubiquitous presence in alcoholic families' lives is collectively denied by their members:

> Imagine an ordinary living room—chairs, couch, coffee table, a TV set, and, in the middle, a LARGE, GRAY EL-EPHANT . . . Imagine also the people who live in this house: a child, along with a mother and/or father and maybe some sisters and brothers. All members of the family have to go through the living room many times each day and the child watches as they walk through the room very . . . carefully . . . around . . . the . . . ELEPHANT. Everyone avoids the swinging trunk and enormous feet. Since no

one ever talks about the ELEPHANT, the child knows
that she's not supposed to talk about it either. And she
doesn't. Not to anyone.[36]

It is precisely elephants' imposing stature and therefore highly
conspicuous presence that accounts for jokes such as "How can
you tell if there's an elephant in your refrigerator? There are
footprints in the butter," or for the scene from the film *Billy
Rose's Dumbo* where someone asks Jimmy Durante about the
elephant he is caught red-handed trying to hide and he replies,
"What elephant?" It is their huge size, of course, that makes the
pathetic efforts to hide them in a refrigerator or behind one's
back so ludicrous.

Like the king's naked body in the story, the proverbial "elephant in the room" is certainly visible to anyone willing to
simply keep one's eyes open. Thus, if anyone fails to notice it, it
can only be as a result of deliberate avoidance, since otherwise
it would be quite impossible *not* to notice it. Indeed, to ignore
an elephant is to ignore the obvious.

The "elephant in the room" is thus metaphorically evocative
of any object or matter of which everyone is definitely aware
yet no one is willing to publicly acknowledge. As such, it has
become the most common cultural representation of the open
secrets around which conspiracies of silence typically revolve.

As if echoing the cartoon on page 12, one member of the House
Budget Committee thus ridicules the seemingly rosy picture of
the state of the United States economy portrayed by President
George W. Bush's economic advisors, essentially noting that
"they all ignored the elephant in the room. They ignored the
fact that [although] the president talk[ed] about getting the
country back on the path to a balanced budget, he was the first
president in recent history to inherit not only a balanced budget but a budget in surplus . . ."[37] Similarly, in an attempt to

© 2003, reprinted with the permission of *The Baltimore Sun*

convey the enormity of the silence surrounding the horrors of
Stalinism, Martin Amis invokes "the elephant—the trumpet-
ing, snorting, farting mammoth—in the Kremlin living room."[38]
The same image has been used to ridicule those who deny any
connection between guns and violence and was likewise invoked
by several political commentators struck by President Bill
Clinton's almost surreal ability to deliver his State of the Union
address less than a week after the Monica Lewinsky scandal broke
out in 1998, not to mention in the middle of his impeachment
trial in 1999:

There was an elephant in the room, but the man at the podium didn't mention it. The allegations about a White House sex scandal sat in the House Chamber like an uninvited pachyderm. Everyone in the room knew it was there, but President Clinton did not want to talk about it. In a 72-minute speech, Clinton discussed everything from Social Security to the Internet, but there wasn't a word about Monica Lewinsky.

Television cameras never picked up the elephant in the room, and President Clinton surely didn't mention it. But that figurative elephant, Clinton's impeachment trial, was everywhere during the president's State of the Union speech Tuesday.

[Having] the impeachment trial and the president's speech hours apart is like having an elephant in the room . . . *It's huge, it's undeniable, yet people pretend it's not there.*[39]

★ ★ ★

As one might expect, what we ignore or avoid socially is often also ignored or avoided academically,[40] and conspiracies of silence are therefore still a somewhat undertheorized as well as understudied phenomenon. Furthermore, they typically consist of nonoccurrences, which, by definition, are rather difficult to observe. After all, it is much easier to study what people do discuss than what they do not (not to mention the difficulty of telling the difference between simply not talking about something and specifically avoiding it).[41]

Yet despite all these difficulties, there have been a number of attempts to study conspiracies of silence. To date, those studies have, without exception, been focally confined to the way we collectively avoid specific topics such as race, homosexuality, the threat of nuclear annihilation, or the Holocaust. But no attempt has yet been made to transcend their specificity in an effort to examine such conspiracies as a general phenomenon.[42] Unfortunately, there is a lack of dialogue between those who study family secrets and those who study state secrets, and feminist writings on silence are virtually oblivious to its nongendered aspects. That naturally prevents us from noticing the strikingly similar manner in which couples, organizations, and even entire nations collectively deny the presence of "elephants" in their midst. Identifying these similarities, however, requires that we ignore the specific contents of conspiracies of silence and focus instead on their formal properties.

The formal features of such conspiracies are revealed when we examine the dynamics of denial at the level of families that ignore a member's drinking problem as well as of nations that refuse to acknowledge the glaring incompetence of their leaders.[43] In an effort to highlight general patterns that transcend any particular social situation, I therefore do not present any in-depth case study of a specific conspiracy of silence. I instead use numerous illustrative examples eclectically drawn from a wide range of substantive contexts. Indeed, the broader the substantive base of evidence on which I draw in my analysis, the greater the generalizability of the observations I can make about the structure and dynamics of collective denial. Throughout the book I therefore deliberately oscillate between widely disparate contexts in order to emphasize the distinctly generic properties of conspiracies of silence. Only by purposefully ignoring superficial differences between seemingly unrelated instances of collective denial, after all, can we actually detect fundamental structural similarities among them. "A book purporting to analyze a universal social process," contends economist Timur Kuran, "must justify its claim to generality by testing its thesis in diverse contexts. It must connect facts previously treated as unrelated by identifying common patterns in geographically distinct, temporally removed, culturally specific events."[44]

I begin by examining the various social norms, conventions, and traditions of attention and communication that actually determine what we consider noteworthy and discussable and what we regard as irrelevant and thereby ignore. I specifically examine institutionalized prohibitions against looking, listening, and speaking that, whether in the form of strict taboos or more subtle rules of tact, help keep certain matters off-limits.

Yet what we notice and what we discuss with others is socially delineated not only by normative pressures to suppress certain information from our awareness or at least refrain from acknowledging its presence, but also by political constraints. Power, after all, involves the ability to control the scope of the information others can access as well as what they pass on and thus promotes various forms of forced blindness, deafness, and muteness. I therefore examine different ways of controlling the scope of others' attention, from formal censorship to informal distraction tactics. In addition, I look at different forms of controlling the scope of their discourse, from formal agenda-setting procedures to informal codes of silence.

I also try to highlight the collaborative nature of conspiracies of silence, noting how each conspirator's actions are symbiotically complemented by the others'. And I examine the factors that make them more effective, showing that the pressure toward silence gains momentum as the number of those who conspire to maintain it increases, the longer it lasts, and when the very act of denial is itself denied.

Yet the presence of the elephant in the room is not always unanimously denied. Indeed, people often try to break conspiracies of silence and make the open secrets around which they revolve part of the public discourse. I examine different forms of breaking the silence ranging from subtle humor to explicit, in-your-face awareness-raising rallies. I also examine public reaction to silence breakers, specifically invoking their opposing roles as innovators and deviants to explain the contrasting responses they typically evoke, namely admiration and resentment. The fact that silence breakers are often resented underscores the considerable benefits of ignoring "elephants." After all, social life presupposes leaving certain things unsaid, and breaking the silence surrounding those things may therefore "rock the boat," destabilizing it. Defying conventional notions of what should actually be noticed as well as discussed with others also undermines some of the basic foundations of social solidarity. Pretending not to notice certain things often helps us save others' face, and dropping such pretense can make our interactions with them considerably awkward.

Yet conspiracies of silence also pose serious problems, and we therefore also need to examine their negative effects on social life. Given the dissonance we almost inevitably experience between what we and others around us seem to notice, conspiracies of silence often lead us to become more distrustful of one another. By promoting some discrepancy between what we actually experience and what we publicly acknowledge, they can also be morally corrosive.

"The best way to disrupt moral behavior," notes political theorist C. Fred Alford, "is not to discuss it and not to discuss not discussing it." "Don't talk about ethical issues," he facetiously proposes, "and don't talk about our not talking about ethical issues."[45] As moral beings we cannot keep on nondiscussing "undiscussables." Breaking this insidious cycle of denial calls for an open discussion of the very phenomenon of undiscussability. This book presents a first systematic attempt to launch such a discussion.

chapter Two

The Rules
of Denial

*The first time she saw a novice faint in the chapel [no] nun or
novice so much as glanced at the white form that had keeled over
from the knees . . . [T]he surrounding sisters seemed to be monsters
of indifference, as removed from the plight of the unconscious one as
though she were not sprawled out blenched before them on the car-
pet. [Then] she realized that she had been staring not at heartless-
ness but at a display of detachment . . . Later on, when she had
trained herself to the exquisite charity of not seeming to see a sister in
torment . . . she would know that few of them ever really reached the
icy peaks of total detachment but only seemed to have done so.*

—Kathryn Hulme, *The Nun's Story*

*B*efore we can begin to explore the structure and dynamics
of conspiracies of silence, we need to look at the cognitive
and behavioral skills that enable us to participate in them. Examining the unmistakably social underpinnings of the acts of
seeing, hearing, and speaking offers us a first glimpse into the
social organization of denial.

Attention and Culture

As we very well know, the proverbial line separating what we notice from what we do not notice is largely a product of various physiological constraints imposed by our sensory organs. Our vision, for example, is confined to a limited "field," and much of what lies beyond our visual horizons never even enters our awareness. Similar physiological constraints restrict what we are able to hear and smell.

Yet how we mentally disembed the "figures" we notice from the surrounding "background" that we essentially ignore is only partly dictated by nature. There is no natural filter, for example, that actually separates the sounds we consider part of a concert (and, therefore, "music") from the many sounds (muffled coughs, squeaking chairs) we so casually tune out as background "noise." Nor is it nature that compels jurors to disregard evidence deemed inadmissible in court.

The way we focus our attention often differs from the way many other people do, yet such variance has little to do with our physiology. Unlike the differences between turtles' and eagles' respective ranges of vision or spiders' and gazelles' respective hearing capacities, the difference between what typically catches tourists' and locals' attention, for example, is not a result of any significant difference in their respective sensory capacities.

The nonphysiological, unmistakably social foundations of the way we pay attention to things are quite evident from the way such attending habits vary among different social groups, and as evident from black girls' greater readiness to talk about sex with their mothers than Latina girls,[1] so do our communicating habits. Thus, whereas some professions explicitly limit the scope of their members' attention, others specifically train them to try to notice "everything," as evident from comparing the highly restrictive style of mental focusing so common among experimental researchers (who are trained to manipulate variables in a pronouncedly decontextualized manner) or surgeons to the way police detectives and investigative reporters, for example, are trained to look for evidence practically "everywhere."

The social underpinnings of what we notice and ignore are also evident from the way it shifts historically. Only a few decades ago smoking, for example, was still considered a "background" activity that, like doodling or drinking coffee, others might not even notice.[2] By the same token, while only two generations ago middle-class Americans still regarded skin color as particularly relevant to their social standing, nowadays they often disregard it altogether. Thus, as social attitudes shift, so does our focus.

Consider also the way traditionally overlooked foci of intellectual concern are suddenly foregrounded academically. As their very name suggests, not until the publication of Freud's *The Psychopathology of Everyday Life* only a little more than a century ago had "Freudian" slips, for example, ever been the subject of a scholarly inquiry. By the same token, not until the publication of Edward Hall's *The Hidden Dimension* in 1966 had anyone ever paid systematic attention to the bubbles of "personal space" with which we surround ourselves when interacting with others.[3]

As evident from looking historically at the amount of exposed female skin that arouses our moral indignation or the number of Americans who are concerned about the hundreds of thousands of Africans who die from starvation almost every year, our moral horizons also keep shifting. Actual legal rights, in fact, are now extended to social categories such as same-sex couples and the unborn, whose legal standing had not even been considered by most people only a few decades ago.[4]

What we consider undiscussable also keeps changing. As Alice Mills and Jeremy Smith note in their book *Utter Silence: Voicing the Unspeakable* about the so-called Starr Report, "Ken Starr's problem is that semen, by the end of the twentieth century, has become all too speakable. Semen, almost unmentionable by anyone but a male doctor at the start of the century, is spoken freely to and by children . . . by the century's end. Speaking semen, for the majority of Starr's readers, carries no sense of breaking a taboo."[5]

Learning to Ignore

Yet while the separation of what we notice from what we ignore is far from strictly natural, nor is it entirely personal.[6] Noticing and ignoring are not just personal acts, since they are always performed by members of particular social communities with particular social conventions of attention and communication.

In fact, the way we focus our attention is often grounded in highly impersonal social traditions of paying attention. So when we notice or ignore something, we therefore often do so as members of particular social communities.[7] Thus, as a twenty-first-century American mortgage broker, for example, one is formally supposed to disregard clients' ethnicity and religious beliefs. By the same token, it is particular social conventions of paying attention that lead us to notice women's breasts while practically ignoring their ears, and particular social traditions of "moral focusing" that lead us to be concerned about some war casualties (women, children, civilians in general) more than others and affect what we come to regard as social problems.[8]

It is hardly a coincidence that the very first person in "The Emperor's New Clothes" to note that the emperor has no clothes is actually a child, who has yet to learn what one is socially supposed not to notice.[9] We normally internalize such traditions of paying attention as part of our socialization.[10] That is where we learn, for example, that we are supposed to disregard applicants' marital status when screening job applications and whether we like particular students when grading their exams. Such socialization may be quite explicit, as evident from the highly formalized "don't ask, don't tell" United States military policy toward homosexuals, although it is usually implicit. By simply watching others ignore certain things we learn to ignore them as well. As she listens to her mother's one-minute account of an entire day they spent together downtown, a young girl tacitly learns what merits social attention and what can actually be ignored. Seeing nobody around her ever mentioning her father's drinking, she likewise learns that it is something one is not supposed to notice.[11]

Needless to say, although one may initially be drawn to a particular profession because it seems to fit one's personal style of mental focusing, the contrast between experimental researchers' and investigative reporters' diametrically opposed focusing habits is most definitely a product of the contrasting manner in which they are professionally socialized to organize their attention. By the same token, if holistic healers are more likely than conventional ear, nose, and throat doctors to also ask patients with ear problems about their neck or shoulders, it is not because they are personally more curious but the result of being professionally socialized to view the entire human body as a single, noncompartmentalized unit.

The considerable extent to which professions' distinctive traditions of paying attention affect what their members notice is particularly evident in science. After all, what scientists actually notice is a product of the specific manner in which they focus their attention as a result of a particular cognitive orientation they acquire as part of their professional socialization.[12] Only by undergoing such socialization do sociologists, for example, acquire the "sociological imagination" that enables them to "see" power structures, labor markets, influence networks, and stratification systems, and only by having done so myself have I developed my own distinctly sociological sensitivity to the collective, normative, and conventional aspects of human cognition.[13] By the same token, as one might suspect, it is their professional socialization that enables radiologists and cardiologists to detect on X-rays and through their stethoscopes early warning signs that others would most likely miss.

When I was in graduate school I was invited once to attend sociologist Robert F. Bales' graduate seminar on group dynamics and, along with his students, observe a small group of people interacting in his social psychology lab. Later, as we compared the notes we had taken while observing them, I noticed that while most of the other students' notes were about the power dynamics within the group, mine revolved mainly around spatial arrangements and performance strategies. Yet the difference between us had little to do with our different personal sensitivities and everything to do with the fact that, unlike them, I was studying at the time with (and greatly influenced by) sociologist Erving Goffman. Goffman's approach to social interaction was quite distinct from Bales', and I was therefore implicitly socialized to observe it quite differently.

Scientists are also professionally socialized to control in their research designs for potentially significant variables they nevertheless choose to systematically disregard. Indeed, part of what distinguishes members of any given academic discipline from those of any other are the variables they tacitly opt to ignore. By holding these variables constant, they thus transform them from potential "figures" into part of the "background" they can actually ignore. When a criminologist decides to examine the relation between offenders' race and the amount of time it takes them to become eligible for parole, for example, such a decision is likely also to entail efforts to systematically ignore their age and marital status, not to mention the nature of their offense. It also presupposes an implicit prior decision on his or her part to regard their reading habits, table manners, and cholesterol level as irrelevant.

The Rules of Irrelevance

There is a considerable difference between merely seeing or hearing (that is, perceiving) something and actually noticing (that is, paying attention to) it, as not everything we experience through our senses always captures our attention.[14] Thus, while engaging in a conversation with someone, for example, we rarely notice the color of the buttons on his shirt despite the fact that they are obviously quite visible. By the same token, during business meetings, we hardly ever notice who takes notes. Many of us are likewise quite oblivious to the small children running around us in picnics and large family get-togethers (which indeed makes them, along with housekeepers and janitors, perfect candidates for spying),[15] and it is not uncommon for parents to even make love in the presence of infants.

Yet ignoring something is more than simply failing to notice it. Indeed, it is quite often the result of some pressure to actively disregard it. Such pressure is usually a product of social norms of attention designed to separate what we conventionally consider "noteworthy" from what we come to disregard as mere background "noise."

Consider, for example, the special "norms of focusing"[16] designed to counteract the nonclinical undertones of the interaction between a woman and her gynecologist. After all, as one astute observer of the peculiar social dynamics of such situations points out, "in the medical world the pelvic area is like any other part of the body [and its] sexual connotations are left behind . . . [Doctors] want it understood that *their gazes take in only medically pertinent facts*, so they are not concerned with an aesthetic inspection of a patient's body."[17] Such norms are embodied in the tacit rules designed to constrain the manner in which those who participate in such situations actually focus their attention. Patients, for example, are thus expected, "to have an attentive glance upward, at the ceiling or at other persons in the room, eyes open, not dreamy or 'away.' [They are] supposed to avoid looking into the doctor's eyes during the actual examination because direct eye contact between the two at this time is provocative."[18]

Similar norms of focusing underlie our ability to mentally separate the persons we consider full-fledged participants in a given social situation from the "nonpersons" such as the above-mentioned small children and janitors whom, although they are physically present there, we nevertheless conventionally ignore.[19] (Indeed, we expect them to "maximally encourage the fiction that they aren't present" and may therefore notice them only when, defying their cognitive marginalization, they actually force themselves into our awareness, as when a kibitzer offers unsolicited advice to chess players or when a cabdriver suddenly joins an ongoing conversation among his passengers.)[20] Such norms of focusing partly also explain why we rarely consciously consider horses, children, or our own siblings sexually attractive. As so memorably portrayed in the hilarious sketch with Gene Wilder and Daisy the sheep in Woody Allen's *Everything You Always Wanted to Know about Sex (But Were Afraid to Ask)*, desiring any member of categories conventionally deemed erotically irrelevant would most likely be considered perverse.[21]

The normative underpinnings of the mental acts of noticing and ignoring are most spectacularly evident in the tacit social rules that determine what we consider irrelevant. After all, separating the "relevant" from the "irrelevant" is a *socio*mental act performed by members of particular social communities who are socialized to focus only on certain parts or aspects of situations while systematically ignoring others.

To appreciate the extent to which noteworthiness is socially delineated in accordance with such "rules of irrelevance," note that, with the possible exception of psychotherapy sessions and first dates, where practically everything is considered relevant, social situations are always surrounded by mental frames designed to help separate what we are socially expected to notice from what we are conventionally supposed to ignore.[22] It is such social conventions of mental framing that lead us to consider, for example, players' weight and gender respectively relevant in boxing and tennis yet utterly ignore them in poker and Parcheesi.[23] They also explain why we are much more likely to notice somebody chewing gum at church than on the subway.

The social foundations of relevance are particularly apparent in bureaucracies, where officials' attention is formally confined to the specific functional niches they occupy and all informal aspects of human relations are deemed irrelevant and, consequently, formally ignored.[24] They are also quite apparent in modern law, as manifested in the way juries are formally instructed and repeatedly reminded to focus their attention exclusively on what is rather restrictively defined as "pertinent" to the case in hand. Thus, under the rape-shield law, for example, plaintiffs' prior sexual history is deemed irrelevant and therefore essentially unmentionable. By the same token, under the exclusionary rule, unlawfully obtained evidence, compelling as it may be, is nevertheless considered inadmissible, and if it is ever brought up in court the judge can actually have it officially stricken off the record and order the jury to disregard it.

Taboo

What society expects us to ignore is often articulated in the form of strict taboos against looking, listening, and speaking. Essentially designed to "keep [our] state of knowledge at a low level" (in fact, the very first prohibition mentioned in the Bible is the one against eating the proverbial fruits of the tree of knowledge),[25] such prohibitions constrain the way we process information. Those who defy or even simply ignore them are considered social deviants and, as such, are the targets of various social sanctions.[26]

Essentially characterized by a strong emphasis on avoidance, these taboos often manifest themselves in the form of strict prohibitions against looking or listening. Thus, among the Australian aborigines, for example, visual as well as aural access to the sacred is strictly forbidden to the profane: "A corpse . . . is sometimes taken out of sight, the face being covered in such a way that it cannot be seen . . . There are ritual songs that women must not hear, on pain of death."[27] The biblical and Greek mythological accounts of the lethal punishment divinely inflicted on Lot's wife and Orpheus for having broken certain taboos against looking are classic examples of efforts made by society to describe the fate of those who choose to ignore or defy its norms of attention by becoming overly curious.

Yet as the familiar image of the three wise monkeys so perfectly reminds us, strict taboos on looking or listening are often coupled with functionally complementary prohibitions against speaking. Thus, on various ceremonial occasions, for example, silence is obligatory, and "if there is talking, it is in a low voice and with the lips only."[28] Furthermore, there are certain things that are never supposed to be discussed, or sometimes even mentioned, at all.

Consider here also the strong taboo, so memorably depicted in films like *Prince of the City*, *Mississippi Burning*, *In the Heat of the Night*, *A Few Good Men*, *Bad Day at Black Rock*, or *Serpico*, against washing one's community's "dirty laundry" in public. Particularly noteworthy in this regard are informal codes of silence such as the omerta, the traditional Sicilian code of honor that prohibits Mafia members from "ratting" on fellow members, or the infamous "blue wall of silence" that, ironically enough, similarly prevents police officers from reporting corrupt fellow officers, not to mention the actual secrecy oaths people must take in order to become members of secret societies or underground movements. Equally prohibitive are the "cultures of silence" that prevent oil workers from reporting oil spills and fraternity members from testifying against fellow brothers facing rape charges, and that have led senior tobacco company executives to suppress the findings of studies showing the incontrovertible health risks involved in smoking, and prevented the typically sensationalist, gossipy British and American press from publicizing the imminent abdication of King Edward VIII in 1936, or the sexual indiscretions of President John F. Kennedy.[29]

A most effective way to make sure that people would actually stay away from conversational "no-go zones"[30] is to keep the tabooed object nameless, as when Catholic preachers, for example, carefully avoid mentioning sodomy (the "nameless sin") by name.[31] It is as if refraining from talking about something will ultimately make it virtually unthinkable, as in the famous dystopian world of George Orwell's *Nineteen Eighty-Four*, where it was practically impossible "to follow a heretical thought further than the perception that it was heretical; beyond that point the necessary words were nonexistent."[32] In fact, the underlying assumption behind the social taboo on the use of various sex-related ("dirty") words is that it is quite possible to actually

eliminate certain ideas by sanitizing our discourse. To quote
Michel Foucault,

> in order to gain mastery over it in reality, it had first been
> necessary to subjugate [sex] at the level of language, con-
> trol its free circulation in speech, expunge it from the things
> that were said, and extinguish the words that rendered it
> too visibly present. And even these prohibitions, it seems,
> were afraid to name it. Without even having to pronounce
> the word, modern prudishness was able to ensure that one
> did not speak of sex, merely through . . . muteness which,
> by dint of saying nothing, imposed silence.[33]

A somewhat milder form of verbal avoidance involves the
use of euphemisms (the "ladies' room," the "F word"), which
allow their users to invoke taboo subjects yet at the same time
avoid mentioning them. Thus, by using euphemisms such as
"medical experiments," one can somewhat indirectly allude to
one's heinous activities as a Nazi doctor in Auschwitz without
ever mentioning them explicitly.[34] By the same token, by using
the rather innocuous brand name "Tampax," advertisers can
actually invoke a highly taboo subject like menstruation while
still keeping it technically undiscussable, which brings to mind
the story about the little boy who, naively enough, wanted to
get the seemingly magical product for his birthday after having
seen on a television commercial that one can do practically anything (swim, bowl, ski, ride a horse, play tennis) with it. Euphemisms are indeed the "deodorant of language," as they
constitute a "code of silent omissions" functionally equivalent
to the "preliminary shower-bath that renders anti-perspirants
unnecessary."[35] That, of course, presupposes the understanding
that they would in fact provide a protective shield rather than
become the very objects of the actual process of shielding, as

one is reminded by the joke about the man who, constantly nagged by his wife to tell their son about "the birds and the bees," finally tells him: "Remember the gentleman and the lady we saw last Sunday behind the trees in the park? Remember what they were doing? Well, the birds and the bees do the same!"

Tact

Yet much of what we are expected to ignore is socially articulated in the even milder form of tact. Although social scientists have yet to even notice the connection between them, tact is but a "soft" version of taboo, and etiquette rules of religious prohibitions. Rules of tact thus usually take the form of subtle ("it might be considered rude") guidelines for polite conduct rather than explicit ("it is strictly forbidden") injunctions. Not surprisingly, unlike taboos, they generally provide us with a somewhat better understanding of the social dynamics of conspiracies of silence generated by embarrassment rather than by fear.

Essentially based on avoidance, such "negative politeness"[36] involves staying away from potentially "sensitive" information one has not been invited to access. As so evocatively captured in the image of the proverbial monkey who hears no evil, that involves certain norms of discourse intended to prevent us from asking other people about "delicate" matters like marital problems, miscarriages, or suicides.[37] Such norms usually take the form of special rules of etiquette designed to keep us from "prying." To quote from a popular guide to "polite" conduct:

> Suppose you go around and find out how old everybody you meet is and how much they paid for their houses. Suppose each person with what you considered a physical oddity informed you in detail why he or she limped . . .

Suppose all single people explained to you why they were single . . . and every adult stated a rationale for the . . . nonexistence of his or her children. Suppose that upon greeting someone, you were able to find out immediately how old each piece of clothing he or she wore was, where it was bought, and for how much . . . [W]hy don't people quit asking such questions at every opportunity and go back to the system in which it was off-bounds to ferret information out of people and each person was allowed to volunteer topics he wished to discuss?[38]

As evident from the way we usually react to "nosy" people who actually do pry, being tactless is generally considered a form of social deviance. Indeed, friends and neighbors may even go as far as to dismiss possible signs of domestic violence (loud altercations, bruises) as private matters one should ignore to avoid being considered nosy.[39]

Needless to say, ignoring someone's stutter, heavy accent, bad breath, or open fly out of politeness is clearly not the result of simply failing to notice it. Nor, for that matter, is it a hearing problem that normally prevents us from eavesdropping on easily overheard conversations taking place around us in a crowded restaurant or a foreign language we are mistakenly presumed not to understand. Indeed, these are all socially expected displays of "civil inattention."[40]

Aside from the pressure to see and hear no evil, there is also a strong social pressure not to acknowledge the fact that we sometimes do indeed see or hear it. Not only are we expected to refrain from asking potentially embarrassing questions, we are also expected to pretend not to have heard potentially embarrassing "answers" even when we actually have. By not acknowledging what we have in fact seen or heard, we can "tactfully" pretend not to have noticed it.

The fact that the verbs "to notice" and "to remark" are denoted in French by a single word (*remarquer*) reminds us how closely related noticing something and publicly acknowledging having noticed it actually are. Yet the fact that in English, by contrast, they nevertheless seem to require two separate words underscores how much those acts are normatively separated from each other. And the difference between what we actually notice and what we publicly acknowledge having noticed is at the very heart of what it means to be tactful.

Being tactful, in other words, often involves pretending not to notice things we "know but realize that [we] are supposed not to know."[41] Thus, one acts tactfully when one "passes over something . . . and leaves it unsaid."[42] As when we forgive someone or pretend to have forgotten the promise he once made to us but never kept, being tactful involves at least outwardly treating things we actually do notice as if they are somehow irrelevant and, as such, can be practically ignored.[43]

More specifically, it often involves trying to ensure that others don't realize we actually do notice certain embarrassing things about them. By acting as if we are somehow "unmindful" of them, we thus try to convey to them that they do not constitute "target[s] of special curiosity" for us, as so poignantly captured in the tongue-in-cheek definition of a polite man as someone who, having mistakenly entered the ladies' showers, quickly apologizes to the naked woman he sees standing there: "Excuse me, sir."[44] Thus, when others make an embarrassing faux pas, for example, we can "feign inattention" and pretend to "tactfully not see" it.[45]

Needless to say, the distinction between tact and taboo is not as clear-cut as it may seem. Indeed, it becomes somewhat fuzzy when one considers, for example, the kind of silence produced by "political correctness," as when people refrain from using race labels to avoid the risk of being considered racist.[46] Such "polite repression"[47] is quite peculiar to social environments and situations lacking clear power structures and some element of coercion. As one might expect, the particular forms of silencing it involves are therefore quite different from the ones one encounters, as we shall now see, in social environments and situations involving clear power relations.

chapter Three

The Politics
of Denial

Repression operated as . . . an injunction to silence . . . an admission that there was nothing to say about such things, nothing to see, and nothing to know.

—Michel Foucault, *The History of Sexuality*

*T*he normative organization of our attention implies a certain amount of consensus about what we should ignore, yet such a consensus may not always exist. The attempts by artists like Edgar Degas (as in *A Woman with Chrysanthemums*), Luigi Pirandello (as in *Tonight We Improvise*),[1] Piet Mondrian (as in *Diamond Painting in Red, Yellow, and Blue*), and John Cage (as in *4'33"*) to challenge the mental frame traditionally separating art from its visual and aural surroundings were self-consciously defiant attacks on conventional attention arrangements,[2] and the debate over whether race ought to be considered a factor in college admissions is essentially a battle over relevance. Heated arguments between lovers over whether one's sexual past is the other's "business"[3] likewise remind us that while some silences may indeed be welcomed by everyone, others may actually be appreciated by some people but not others.

Thus far we have looked at the normative pressures that help generate conspiracies of silence, yet the social pressure to ignore certain things is only partly produced by norms. The scope of our attention and discourse is socially delineated by normative as well as political constraints, and what we see, hear, and talk about is affected by both normative and political pressures. Only when we examine the political conditions that help produce conspiracies of silence can we understand why it is the emperor's lack of clothing (and not, say, one of his attendants') that so dramatically captures the essence of the so-called elephant in the room in "The Emperor's New Clothes."

Attention and Power

A first step in this direction would be to examine the role of power in the social organization of our attention and discourse. After all, social relations usually involve power, and silence and denial are often products of the way it is asymmetrically distributed among us.[4]

What we are aware of is partly a function of how much power we have. As evident from the way access to "confidential" (not to mention "top secret") and "unclassified" information is formally institutionalized in terms of different levels of security clearance, for example, different levels of awareness often correspond to different positions of power.

Power also enables people to control the amount of information that is conveyed to them. Thus, if information is conveyed informally, it is possible to feign ignorance later and avoid being held accountable if possessing it becomes a liability. After all, it is far more expedient not to know, for example, about certain wrongdoings and avoid risking complicity by failing to report them. Higher-ups may thus ask to be kept "fully and tightly *un*informed" (and thereby officially "out of the loop") about illegal activities of which they are in fact quite aware to avoid liability. John Mitchell would indeed refrain from ever mentioning any Watergate-related matters to Richard Nixon in order to keep him "antiseptically unaware" and thus out of legal trouble.[5]

Yet power also entails a wider scope of attention, as exemplified by the hierarchical organization of levels of focusing according to social rank.[6] A brigade commander is thus expected to have broader concerns than the commanders of his battalions, who, in turn, are expected to have a somewhat broader perspective than the commanders of their companies. That explains, for example, why only a handful of very senior FBI officers could have possibly "connected the dots" provided by the bureau's Phoenix and Minneapolis offices prior to the September 11 attacks on the World Trade Center and the Pentagon.

Needless to say, it is formal role expectations rather than a personal lack of curiosity that lead company commanders to approach military situations tactically rather than strategically. Nor would we normally attribute university presidents' and regular faculty's notably different levels of knowledge and concern about university-wide matters to their different levels of personal curiosity about them.

Yet even more critical than the fact that power entails a wider scope of attention is the fact that it also involves the ability to control the scope of *others'* attention. Through the required readings they assign it is thus teachers, for example, who determine what students regard as noteworthy rather than the other way around. And when lawyers try to claim the court's attention by interjecting an objection, it is the judge who has the authority to decide whether to sustain or overrule it.

Power also involves control over the bounds of acceptable discourse. After all, it is usually superiors who tell their subordinates "Let's not talk about that."[7] It was a subtle political battle over the power to delineate the scope of their discourse, for example, that prompted Russian president Vladimir Putin, when he was asked by George W. Bush to join his war effort against Iraq, to point out the far greater role of longtime United States allies Saudi Arabia and Pakistan in promoting Islamist terrorism around the world.[8]

The most common way of gaining control over the scope of others' attention and discourse is by controlling the "agenda." As exemplified by the political dynamics of establishing what is included on (and thus implicitly also what is excluded from) a meeting's agenda and thereby formally defining what is "on the table," it is normally superiors who determine what their subordinates regard as relevant rather than the other way around. Similarly, through their power to set the "national agenda," it is national leaders who determine the amount of public attention respectively given to health care, education, and national security.

Furthermore, power also involves the ability to redirect others' attention by "changing the subject." Indeed, leaders often create crises (and may even start wars) to distract public attention from economic problems or political scandals. (Some of George W. Bush's critics have in fact explicitly portrayed Iraq's alleged weapons of mass destruction as "weapons of mass distraction" or, invoking a famous Hitchcockian tactic of diverting viewers' attention away from a film's main plot, as "MacGuffins of mass destruction.")[9] Like professional magicians, they also time unpopular or potentially embarrassing acts such as announcing controversial appointments or firing senior aides to coincide with other events that would conveniently overshadow them.

It is the attention-grabbing power of the mass media, of course, that enables leaders to "capture" an entire nation's attention (and with radio or television even to get it to jointly focus on the same thing at the same time).[10] In fact, it is the media who determine what is actually displayed on our collective radar screen, and though they may not always be successful in telling us what to think, they are "stunningly successful in telling [us] what to think *about*."[11] Furthermore, by determining which issues and events make newspaper headlines and become the lead stories on radio and television newscasts they obviously also determine their perceived public relevance.[12]

Needless to say, the media also help keep various things out of our awareness by simply not covering them. That is in fact true not only in totalitarian societies, where all the television networks, radio stations, and newspapers are controlled by the government, but also in pronouncedly pluralistic political systems, as when most of the American press almost collusively refrains from covering "minor" candidates it believes (and in a self-fulfilling manner thereby also ensures) would not play a major role in an upcoming election,[13] which certainly underscores the tremendous political significance of "alternative" news.

As a matter of fact, the media also determine how long public attention actually lasts, as evident from the way we often follow a particular news story for several weeks only to practically forget about it once media coverage ends. There is a normal media-driven communal attention cycle whereby a particular issue or event enters the public's awareness, stays there for some time, and then gradually fades. A "crime wave" may thus reflect a certain change in our collective awareness of crime as a result of media coverage rather than in the actual crime rate.[14] After all, even major news items tend to recede to less prominent spots on our public radar screen after a while and eventually drop off it altogether, as exemplified by the announcement at the bottom of the 21 April 2003 front page of the *New York Times* that "Coverage of the Iraq war and its aftermath, which has occupied a separate section in recent weeks, returns to the regular news pages today, beginning on Page A10." The politics of agenda setting are also quite spectacularly evident in the way scholarly attention and conversation are socially organized. Like school curricula and history textbooks,[15] a list of required readings for a doctoral exam exemplifies the power to determine what others must be aware of and what they can basically ignore. No less significant, however, are more subtle forms of "sociomental control"[16] such as the tacit norms of academic attention and conversation that compel scholars to incorporate in their work a certain body of "literature" with which they are professionally expected to be responsibly familiar. By merely skimming the bibliography of a recent article, let alone reading a featured "review essay," young scholars are thus tacitly pressured to regard certain works as "must reads" while disregarding unmentioned ones as practically irrelevant.

Scholars are also socially pressured to confine their intellectual attention to certain conventional zones of academic discourse ("fields," "disciplines," or even more narrowly designated "areas" of specialization within them) and to regard any scholarly activity taking place outside them as professionally tangential, if not irrelevant. Using various incentives and disincentives, my professional community thus constantly pressures me to keep my scholarly concerns within the bounds of what it considers "sociology" and tacitly discourages me from undertaking any "historical," "psychological," or "anthropological" research project, for example.

Specifically designed to delimit the scopes of academic attention and discourse and keep intellectual thoroughbreds "focused," such institutional blinders are the reason so few scholars today actually transcend the confines of their inherently parochial mental ghettos and venture in their reading and writing into intellectual turfs conventionally regarded as other than their own. Those who ignore such social pressure often face considerable difficulties getting hired, promoted, funded, and published—a most unfortunate outcome given that the cognitive ability to integrate conventionally separate mental realms is one of the hallmarks of human creativity.[17]

Mind Your Own Business

Power also involves the ability to control (which may sometimes actually include blocking) others' access to information. After all, it is normally parents who tell their children rather than children who tell their parents what books they can or cannot read and what television shows they can or cannot watch.

Blocking others' access to information may involve formal acts of censorship such as closing newspapers and radio stations, taking a television program off the air, or banning a history textbook. Yet it can also be done in a much less formal manner through "friendly suggestions" like "Don't ask too many questions" or "Mind your own business." As Nixon's campaign finance chairman replied when the treasurer of the Committee to Re-Elect the President asked him about the money paid to the Watergate "plumbers," "I do not want to know and you do not want to know."[18]

As one might expect, blocking people's access to information is one of the hallmarks of the police state. Thus, throughout Nazi-occupied Europe, listening to Allied radio stations, for example, was strictly prohibited, and people who lived near concentration camps were actually ordered by the SS to ignore the atrocities that were committed right before their eyes. Specifically forbidden to stare at inmates or even watch the trains that transported them to the camp, they were explicitly instructed to turn their heads away or lower their gaze. When passing by the camp's barracks, anxious parents would often tell their children, "Don't look, don't listen."[19]

Needless to say, such harsh censorship also requires considerable self-censoring, which usually involves "knowing what not to know."[20] Thus, despite the fact that the Nazi deportations of German Jews to Eastern Europe were often carried out in public (not to mention the widespread rumors about what awaited them there), many Germans "knew enough to know that it was better not to know more." By the same token, although people who lived near the death camps could clearly identify the unmistakable source of the smoke and the stench coming out of the crematoria, they nevertheless avoided asking "unnecessary" questions and, feigning ignorance, by and large tried to "look innocent by not noticing."[21] (Unlike tactful, "civil" inattention, however, this was clearly motivated by fear and designed to protect oneself rather than save someone else's face.) In other words, they pretended "to ignore what they otherwise could not help but notice. [They] learned that if awareness of what was happening in and around the camp was unavoidable, one might still look away. Although cognizant of the terror in the camp, they learned to walk a narrow line between unavoidable awareness and prudent disregard."[22] In so doing, they thus came to embody "the type [of citizen who makes the authoritarian] regime possible: *not speaking, not looking, not even asking afterward, not once curious.*"[23]

Button Your Lip

Yet social pressures against being curious are usually complemented by equally prohibitive pressures to be discreet. After all, power involves the ability to block not only initial access to information but also its further circulation. Hush money, for example, always flows down the power ladder, and comments like "this should stay between us" (or "in this room") are typically made by superiors to their subordinates rather than the other way around.

Furthermore, silencing is also used "as a weapon of subjugation . . . the suffocation of the Other's voice." Thus, during Argentina's infamous "Dirty War" against its political dissidents in the late 1970s and early 1980s, any discussion of "disappearances" one may have witnessed was strictly prohibited by the authorities—"a sad example of double silencing. First, a group of individuals is kidnapped and there is no record of their tragic fate, and then their existence is tabooed so that no genuine talk about them is possible." Specifically designed to disempower people, such prohibitive silence also surrounded the Nazi and Soviet concentration and labor camps and is indeed one of the hallmarks of the totalitarian police state, as so chillingly portrayed by Orwell: "Syme had vanished. A morning came, and he was missing from work; a few thoughtless people commented on his absence. On the next day, nobody mentioned him . . . Syme had ceased to exist; he had never existed."[24]

Freely circulating information destabilizes existing power structures. As so strikingly exemplified by the phenomenon of blackmail, one's mere ability to spread potentially damaging information about one's superior can fundamentally subvert the existing power dynamics between them. The very possibility that she might someday tell someone about their illicit affair gives even a lowly secretary considerable power over a seemingly omnipotent boss.

Secrecy helps prevent such implicitly subversive scenarios. By keeping certain information from becoming public,[25] it is designed to make people who have it less threatening, thereby tacitly stabilizing existing power structures. As Strom Thurmond's

mortified family greeted a retired African-American school-
teacher's nationally publicized announcement that she was the
late archsegregationist senator's illegitimate daughter, "For
something to be done so publicly . . . well, we're just not com-
fortable dealing with things in that way . . . There should have
been a private conversation."[26]

Secrecy can be formally mandated, as exemplified by the special confidentiality agreements designed to prevent domestic
staff from divulging kiss-and-tell information about celebrities'
private lives, or the aptly named "gag orders" that keep people
from disclosing legally confidential information other than on
a "need-to-know" basis (the vague definition of which implicitly promotes a more vigilant and therefore nondiscriminatory
silence). Equally prohibitive are the secret settlements designed
to protect offenders by preemptively blocking future circulation of incriminating information about them—a perfectly legal form of essentially bribing victims in exchange for their
silence.

Needless to say, although victims certainly benefit from them
financially and sometimes also reputationally, it is almost always the perpetrators of those wrongdoings who "insist on in-
serting confidentiality clauses in [secret] settlements—never the
victims."[27] Furthermore, the fact that the very existence of those
settlements is often kept secret actually allows such wrongdo-
ing to continue! Such secrecy implicitly empowers repeat offenders by sanctioning the isolation of their victims from one
another, victims who are often unaware that those perpetrators
have previously been accused of similar offenses: "The main
loser in secret settlements is the public. Consumers are deprived
of information they need to protect themselves from unsafe
products. Workers are kept in the dark about unsafe working
conditions . . . In 1933 the Johns Manville company settled a

lawsuit by 11 employees who had been made sick by asbestos. If that settlement had not been kept secret for 45 years, thousands of other workers might not have contracted respiratory diseases."[28] Similarly, when such settlements are used, for example, to protect a pedophile priest, his victims are unlikely to know that they are part of a larger general pattern of abuse. Instead, believing that they are alone, they view their own victimization as highly idiosyncratic and may even blame themselves in part for what happened.

Indeed, it is such secrecy that has made it possible for Church authorities to reassign such serial predators to other parishes, thereby allowing them to continue molesting still more unsuspecting young victims:

> One of the most troubling . . . aspects of the child sexual abuse scandal now roiling the Roman Catholic Church is the enabling role played by the court system. In case after case, judges have signed off on secret settlements of child-molestation suits, freeing the offending priests to molest again . . . One Boston judge who sealed court records in a priest molestation case [said] that she might not have done so "if I had been aware of how widespread this issue was." It was, of course, rulings like hers . . . that helped hide just how big a problem sex abuse was in the church.[29]

> [T]here is palpable unease . . . about the cumulative effect of so many secret agreements. "I'm ashamed I took their money now," said Raymond P. Sinibaldi, who won a settlement from the church in 1995 after allegedly being abused by a priest . . . "I should have . . . filed a lawsuit and called a press conference to announce it. If we had done that, this problem would have been exposed long ago."[30]

Needless to say, it is precisely this "divide-and-rule" aspect of secrecy that Megan's Law and similar other efforts to ban secret settlements are designed to offset.[31]

Yet as common expressions such as "button your lip" or "hold your tongue" remind us, it is more often informal pressures than formal gag orders and secret settlements that actually keep "sensitive" information from spreading. Such pressures sometimes involve displays of physical force, as when rapists literally gag their victims to prevent them from calling for help, or when actual cages with spiked iron plates were placed over gossip-mongers' heads and tongues in seventeenth-century England.[32] However, they usually take the form of verbal threats such as the ones often made against assault victims by the assailant or a fellow victim to never tell anyone what happened. As Tom Wingo recounts the aftermath of being raped along with his mother and sister in Pat Conroy's *The Prince of Tides*, "before my father came home, my mother had gathered us together in the living room and extracted a promise from each of us that we would never tell a living soul what had happened to our family that day . . . [S]he told us that she would cease being our mother if we broke that promise. She swore that she would never speak to us again if we revealed a single detail of that terrible day."[33] By the same token, in an effort to convince the Spanish crown that on his second voyage to America he had actually reached China, Christopher Columbus threatened to cut out the tongues of any of his crew members who ever testified that he never did prove that Cuba was indeed part of the Asian mainland as he claimed.[34]

Yet the pressure to keep something secret is usually more subtle. "Go in there and read this," says the commanding general in the film *Command Decision* as he hands a reporter a classified file, "then forget what you've read." By the same token, following a rather embarrassing jealous outburst by Monica

Lewinsky that was witnessed by several White House Secret Service officers, President Clinton needed only to tell their commander "I hope you use your discretion." The commander then told those officers in an equally subtle manner that "Whatever just happened didn't happen."[35]

Consider also, in this regard, the way in which the two swindlers in "The Emperor's New Clothes" manage to preemptively silence anyone who might give away their secret by proclaiming their imaginary fabric to have "the strange quality of being invisible to anyone who [is] unfit for his office or unforgivingly stupid."[36] As so memorably portrayed in the film *The Fallen Idol*, one can rather similarly prevent children from reporting illicit incidents they happen to witness by seductively presenting them to them as highly exclusive information to which only they are privy.

Indeed, imposing secrecy need not involve any verbal exchange at all, as when a potential witness is promoted or given a raise in tacit exchange for his or her silence, or when a child molester simply closes the blinds or locks the door.[37] Needless to say, silencing is often done in utter silence.

chapter Four

The Social Structure of Denial

It only takes one person to produce speech, but it requires the cooperation of all to produce silence.

—Robert E. Pittenger et al., *The First Five Minutes*

The Double Wall of Silence

*A*s we approach denial from a sociological rather than a more traditional psychological perspective, we soon realize that it usually involves more than just one person and that we are actually dealing with "co-denial," a social phenomenon involving more than just individuals.[1] In order to study conspiracies of silence we must first recognize, therefore, that, whether it is only a couple of friends or a large organization, they always involve an entire social system.

Co-denial presupposes mutual avoidance. Only when the proverbial elephant in the room is jointly avoided by everyone around it, indeed, are we actually dealing with a "conspiracy" of silence.

47

As the foremost expression of co-denial, silence is a collective endeavor, and it involves a collaborative effort on the parts of both the potential generator and recipient of a given piece of information to stay away from it. "Unlike the activity of speech, which does not require more than a single actor, silence demands collaboration."[2] A conspiracy of silence presupposes discretion on the part of the non-producer of the information as well as inattention on the part of its non-consumers. It is precisely the collaborative efforts of those who avoid mentioning the elephant in the room and those who correspondingly refrain from asking about it that make it a conspiracy.

To fully understand the social dynamics of co-denial we therefore need to revisit our three little monkeys. Although at first glance it is only the one who speaks no evil who seems to be in any way responsible for generating silence, a more nuanced view of both silence and denial would require that we also consider its two partners and carefully examine the relations among the three of them.

Consider, for example, the symbiotic relation between the acts of not speaking and not hearing,[3] as so perfectly embodied in the subtle relations between secrecy and tact. After all, in order for Bill Clinton to be able to keep his illicit affair with Monica Lewinsky secret, it was also critical that people around him would not be, at least openly, too curious about it. Thus, though somewhat suspicious about the nature of their relationship, his personal secretary, Betty Currie, for instance, nevertheless tried hard to "avoid learning the details." Even Treasury Secretary Robert Rubin, who was officially supposed to oversee the activities of the White House Secret Service, made a conscious effort not to find out what its agents actually knew about the affair. "I [didn't] have any interest in the facts," he later explained. In fact, he added, "I wouldn't sit in the same room if they wanted to tell me."[4]

Later, as he tried to cover up the widely publicized fact that he had actually quite literally had no clothes, the American emperor was likewise counting on people around him to display the kind of tactful incuriosity exhibited by Steven Spielberg, who later claimed that "I never came out and asked him if it was true, so he never had to lie to me. Whenever we were together, we talked about family and all sorts of stuff, but we never talked about the elephant in the room."[5] By the same token, as he delivered his State of the Union address only a few days after the scandal broke out in 1998 and in the middle of his impeachment trial in 1999, he relied on his audience's sense of decorum and their willingness to tactfully pretend to be unaware of the highly embarrassing circumstances in which it was delivered.

Furthermore, as one is reminded by the discreet manner in which Thomas Jefferson conducted his illicit relationship with his slave Sally Hemings, which in effect also allowed his family to avoid having to acknowledge its existence, being tactful toward others presupposes some preventive display of tact on their part as well. After all, if others expect me to (at least pretend to) ignore them, they also need to be particularly careful not to force themselves on my attention. Indeed, it is much easier to hear no evil when others speak no evil, and also to see no evil when they "show no evil," as exemplified by the collaborative manner in which society's general discomfort with nudity is jointly expressed by seemingly incurious non-voyeurs and modest non-exhibitionists. By being discreet we actually help others avoid embarrassing us.[6]

The "equal protection" provided to those who show no evil as well as to those who see no evil is the result of the symmetrical nature of the relations between the opposing social forces underlying conspiracies of silence. Such symmetry is evident even in highly asymmetrical relations, as so perfectly exemplified by the reluctance of both children and parents to discuss sexual matters with one another, the former feeling uncomfortable asking (and later telling) and the latter feeling equally uncomfortable telling (and later asking). Consider also the remarkable symmetry between someone's wish to keep some atrocity secret and another's urge to deny its reality even to oneself, as exemplified by the symbiotic relations between the politically incurious Alicia and her ever-evasive husband Roberto in the film *The Official Story*. Or note the chillingly symmetrical dynamics of silence between the fearsome perpetrators and the fearful witnesses of these atrocities, as exemplified by the Nazis' efforts to hide the horrors of their concentration camps from nearby residents who in turn willingly turned a blind eye to their existence.[7]

By collaboratively seeing and showing, or hearing and speaking, no evil we thus construct a "double wall" of silence, originally theorized by psychologist Dan Bar-On in the context of the relations between former Nazi perpetrators and their children yet, ironically, equally central to the dynamics between their victims and *their* children. After all, the heavy silence hanging over many Holocaust survivors' homes is a product of "the interweaving of two kinds of conflicted energy: on the part of the survivor, [the] suppression of telling; on the part of the descendant, [the] fear of finding out." (As one child of survivors recalls, talking about the Holocaust "was never overtly forbidden. By no means was I or my brother ever shushed when we attempted to steer the conversation [there]. We simply never made such attempts.") That explains how someone may indeed remain forever unclear as to who actually prevented her mother from telling her how her grandmother was killed: "I don't know whether the stopping of the conversation was my own doing or hers." It was most likely both.[8]

As so explicitly articulated in the United States military's "don't ask, don't tell" policy, the proverbial closet often surrounding

town elders so persistently ignore Tiresias' explicit denunciation of Oedipus as the person who killed Laius?[11]

As we are so artfully reminded by Sophocles, parent-child
incest involves more than just a parent and a child. In families
where a child is sexually molested by a parent there is usually
another parent who collaborates by ignoring it (in the same way
that sexual abuse by a priest often also involves a supposedly
supervising bishop who looks the other way). By the same token, although wife battering technically involves only the
batterer, who tries to keep it secret, and his victim, who feels
too embarrassed to tell anyone about it, the silence surrounding it often also involves other family members, neighbors, and
friends who are quite aware of it yet somewhat reluctant to no-
tify the authorities.

Denying the Denial

Almost paradoxically, silence is often covered up by sound. So-
called small talk, nervous chatter, and "beating around the bush"
are but different forms of "conspiracies of noise"[12] specifically
designed to cover up uncomfortable silences. (So is "background" music. It was the haunting image of the band that kept
on playing while the *Titanic* was sinking that must have inspired
Randy Shilts to title his chronicle of the silence-ridden AIDS
epidemic of the 1980s *And the Band Played On*.) When there is
an elephant in the room, we often find "some subject other
than what is happening" to talk about.[13]

Yet what makes conspiracies of silence even more insidious
than covering it up is the fact that the silence itself is never actually discussed among the conspirators. Unlike when we explicitly agree not to talk about something ("let's not get into

homosexuality is remarkably similar both structurally and fur tionally. Fundamentally double-walled, it is essentially "a co laborative construction of gay and straight" built by both of the together. After all, contrary to common belief, it is "not just shield . . . that prevents those outside it from hearing," as it also "prevents those [inside] it from speaking."[9]

Consider also the double wall of silence jointly constructed by doctors and terminal patients around the patient's imminent death, when "both doctor and patient know of the latter's fatal illness, and both know the other knows, but they do not talk to each other about it" as "the physician does not care to [discuss it] and the patient does not press the issue." Tacit "you don't tell and I don't ask" agreements also exist between spouses where she "doesn't comment on the looks he gives younger women" while he "never mentions his suspicion that she fakes orgasms," or when they try (as so effectively portrayed in the film *The Secret Lives of Dentists*) to tactfully explain away each other's evasive or deceptive accounts of his or her whereabouts instead of openly "exposing [his or her] subterfuge."[10]

Yet walls of silence are often more than double, since the number of those who participate in such conspiracies is by no means limited to two. Consider, for example, the various co-conspirators who help keep Oedipus unaware of having killed his father and married his own mother in Sophocles' classic study of co-denial, *Oedipus Rex*. After all, when investigating Laius' death, why does Creon, for example, never send for the one surviving eyewitness who can actually identify Oedipus, the man who killed him? By the same token, in their 17 years together, why does Jocasta fail to make the almost self-evident connection between her considerably younger husband's badly deformed feet (from the Greek word for which his very name is derived) and her own foot-pierced son, who would have actually been exactly his age if he were still alive? And why do the that"), the very fact that the conspirators avoid it remains unacknowledged and the subtle social dynamics underlying their silence are thus concealed. "It is like the tale of the emperor's new clothes. Everyone understands that it is risky to speak . . . but this fact itself is 'undiscussable.'"[14] A perfect example of such silence about silence, or meta-silence, is the secrecy typically surrounding secrets. As Mark Jordan has so insightfully observed, "if there is any one 'secret' of Catholic clerical homosexuality, it is the urgent anxiety that there is something unknown, something frightening, that must be kept hidden. It is the fearful effort behind the various arrangements for keeping secrets. The 'secret' is the effort itself."[15]

Indeed, the reason it is so difficult to talk about the elephant in the room is that "not only does no one want to listen, but no one wants to talk about not listening."[16] In other words, the very act of avoiding the elephant is itself an elephant! Not only do we avoid it, we do so without acknowledging that we are actually doing so, thereby denying our denial.

Like "rules against seeing rules against seeing," being "forbidden to talk about the fact that we are forbidden to talk" about certain things, or the fact that "we do not see what we prefer not to, and do not see that we do not see," such meta-denial presupposes a particular form of self-deception famously identified by Orwell as "doublethinking," or the ability "consciously to induce unconsciousness, and then . . . to become unconscious of the act of hypnosis you had just performed." Thus, in *Nineteen Eighty-Four*, when Eastasia suddenly assumes Eurasia's traditional role as Oceania's perpetual enemy and the Oceanians set out to immediately destroy or rectify any references ever made to their long-lasting war with Eurasia, Orwell astutely observes that "the work was overwhelming, all the more so because the processes that it involved could not be called by their true names."[17]

Bystanders and Enablers

Having identified the social system as the logical context for studying conspiracies of silence, let us examine the structural features of social relations and social situations that most significantly affect the likelihood of participating in one. We thus need to compare, for example, relations among equals to ones that involve power, public situations to private ones, and so on.

As we might expect, the likelihood of participating in a conspiracy of silence is greatly affected by one's proximity to the proverbial elephant. The closer one gets to it, the more pressure one feels to deny its presence. Indeed, it is the people standing in the street and watching the royal procession rather than those who are actually part of it who are the first ones to break through the wall of denial and publicly acknowledge that the emperor has in fact no clothes.[18]

Just as significant is the effect of social proximity among those standing around the elephant. After all, the socially "closer" we are, the more we tend to trust, and therefore the less likely we are to refrain from talking more openly with, one another. Formal relations and the social environments that foster them (such as bureaucracy), on the other hand, are more likely to discourage openness and thereby promote silence.

Equally significant is the political "distance" between us. We generally tend to trust our equals more than our superiors. Social systems with particularly hierarchical structures and thus more pronounced power differences therefore produce greater reluctance toward openness and candor.

Yet the one structural factor that most dramatically affects the likelihood of participating in conspiracies of silence is the actual number of conspirators involved. In marked contrast to ordinary secrets, the value of which is a direct function of their exclusivity (that is, of the paucity of people who share them),[19] open secrets actually become more tightly guarded as more, rather than fewer, people are "in the know." Indeed, the larger the number of participants in the conspiracy, the "heavier" and more "resounding" the silence. Prohibiting strictly one-on-one encounters such as Winston and Julia's illicit rendezvous in *Nineteen Eighty-Four* may thus be the most effective way for a dystopian police state to ensure that certain things are never openly discussed.

As famously demonstrated by one of the founding fathers of modern sociology, Georg Simmel, one only needs to compare social interactions among three as opposed to two persons to appreciate the extent to which the dynamics of social interactions are affected by the number of participants involved in them. And indeed, unlike two-person conspiracies of silence, even ones involving only three conspirators already presuppose the potential presence of a new key player in the social organization of denial, namely the silent bystander.[20]

As so chillingly portrayed in the film *The Incident*, two young hoodlums actually terrorize an entire subway car not despite, but precisely because of, the presence of so many passengers jointly watching them and, through their silence, effectively restraining one another from acting to stop them. No wonder we often regard silent bystanders as enablers who, by implicitly exemplifying the undiscussability of atrocities and abuse, enable their denial. Women who remain silent in the face of husbands or boyfriends who molest their daughters help perpetuate the abuse by the very fact that they so persistently refrain from explicitly acknowledging it. So, for that matter, do one's friends, relatives, and co-workers who look the other way and pretend not to notice obvious signs of one's alcohol or other drug addiction.[21]

Silent bystanders act as enablers because watching others ignore something encourages one to deny its presence. As evident from studies that show how social pressure affects our perception, it is psychologically much more difficult to trust one's senses and remain convinced that what one sees or hears is actually there when no one else around one seems to notice it. The discrepancy between others' apparent inability to notice it and one's own sensory experience creates a sense of ambiguity that further increases the likelihood that one would ultimately succumb to the social pressure and opt for denial.[22]

Such pressure is further compounded as the number of silent bystanders increases. As Dr. Tomas Stockmann, a brave, relentless fighter against denial, is bound to discover in Henrik Ibsen's play *An Enemy of the People*, "the worst enemy to truth . . . is the majority."[23] The more people I see ignoring the elephant in the room, the harder it is for me to remain convinced that it is indeed standing there, as my own senses tell me. And the situation of being in a minority, constantly resisting the majority's pressure to join the conspiracy and ignore it, inevitably becomes more pronounced as the number of those silent conspirators increases. As we very well know, broaching an unmentionable subject is much more daunting when there are 30 rather than just three other people around, none of whom seems eager to discuss it.

Moreover, the actual experience of watching several other people ignore the elephant together is significantly different from watching each of them ignore it by himself, because it involves the added impact of observing each of them watch the others ignore it as well! Instead of several isolated individuals in denial, one is thus surrounded by a group of people who are obviously all participating in one and the same conspiracy. Furthermore, moving from two- to three-person, let alone wider, conspiracies of silence involves a significant shift from a strictly interpersonal kind of social pressure to the collective kind we call group pressure, whereby breaking the silence actually violates not only some individuals' personal sense of comfort, but a collectively sacred social taboo, thereby evoking a heightened sense of fear.

Along similar lines, notice the difference between private and public communication. The information shared with a close friend about one's marital problems is rarely meant for public consumption. By the same token, while co-workers may quite readily discuss higher-ups' corrupt or incompetent behavior "behind the safety of closed doors and in veiled whispers . . . only the foolish or naive dare to speak of it in public" (which also explains why the norms of "political correctness" are much more likely to be breached in restroom graffiti than in public lectures or on television).[24]

Silence Like A Cancer Grows

As they unfold in time, conspiracies of silence seem to follow a particular trajectory. For a complete picture of such conspiracies we therefore need to also examine their highly patterned social dynamics.[25]

In "The Emperor's New Clothes," although neither the prime minister nor the emperor's other trusted councilor can actually see the nonexistent fabric, they nevertheless presume that everyone else besides them, including the emperor, can, and therefore praise it profusely to protect their reputation. Their utterly disingenuous testimony, however, in turn leads the emperor to conclude that *he* must be the only one who cannot see it. "'What!' thought the emperor," looking at the empty loom, "'I can't see a thing! Why, this is a disaster! Am I stupid? Am I unfit to be emperor?'" And yet "aloud he said, 'It is very lovely,'" thereby practically helping perpetuate a vicious cycle of inevitably erroneous assumptions. Thus, as the story continues, "all the councilors, ministers, and men of great importance . . . stared and stared [and] saw no more than the emperor had seen," yet they nevertheless "said the same thing that he had said, 'It is lovely.'"[26] By the same token, when one staff member witnesses another disregard an overtly audible statement in a meeting, for example, the impression that it is irrelevant may be mutually reinforced by the second staff member's disregard. Indeed, a vicious cycle may be generated in which each conspirator's denial bolsters the others', their collective silence thereby increasingly reverberating as yet a third and then a fourth person join the conspiracy. "Silence," notes Paul Simon, "like a cancer grows,"[27] which is indeed how an entire society may come to collectively deny its leaders' incompetence, glaring atrocities, and impending environmental disasters.

The intensity of silence is thus affected not only by the number of people who conspire to maintain it but also by the length of time they manage to do so. As evident from the rather common lack of communication between longtime couples about the quality of their sex life, silence can be quite "heavy" even in two-person social interaction if it lasts long enough. Indeed, despite the likelihood that a silence would be interrupted the longer it lasts, it instead tends to become more prohibitive as time goes on.

This is largely a result of the inherently cumulative nature of silence. Like any other form of denial (as anyone who has ever been in psychotherapy must know), silence is self-reinforcing, and the longer we remain silent, the more necessary it therefore becomes "to cover [our] silence with further silence."[28] Today's silence will make it harder to break tomorrow.

As Samuel Johnson once said, "*silence propagates itself* [and] the longer talk has been suspended the more difficult it is to find anything to say." By the same token, "the longer [things] remain undiscussed, the harder it becomes to talk about them." Indeed, as we are sadly reminded by reading Jane Smiley's *A*

Thousand Acres, it may actually take two sisters some 20 years before they feel ready (that is, if they ever do at all) to share with each other their common memories of being molested by their father.[29]

Indeed, "elephants" usually grow with time, their figurative size hence reflecting their age. The longer we pretend not to notice them, the larger they loom in our minds. As a child of Holocaust survivors describes the silence surrounding his parents' traumatic past, "every year [it] grew taller [and] I came to be more and more aware of its presence, and of how odd it was that we never spoke of it, since it dominated the landscape."[30]

Given this, how long can people keep pretending not to notice the elephant in the room before it becomes too large (and its presence, therefore, too obvious) to credibly ignore? Is there, in fact, anything that can stop such seemingly endless spiral of denial? Indeed, what actually *does* bring conspiracies of silence to an end?

chapter Five

Breaking the Silence

> *"But he doesn't have anything on!" cried a little child. "Listen to the innocent one," said the proud father. And the people whispered among each other and repeated what the child had said. "He doesn't have anything on. There's a little child who says that he has nothing on." "He has nothing on!" shouted all the people at last.*
>
> —Hans Christian Andersen,
> "The Emperor's New Clothes"

*P*aradoxically, although the pressure to participate in conspiracies of silence increases as they become larger and longer, the opportunities to end them increase as well. In other words, as the silence becomes heavier there are also more chances that it will be broken. Indeed, as the way "The Emperor's New Clothes" ends seems to suggest, if even a single person is unwilling to deny the elephant's presence, he may ultimately lead an entire group of conspirators to acknowledge it publicly.

Furthermore, even if none of the conspirators ever actually breaks the silence, there is always a chance that they might, which makes even a potential silence breaker an integral part of any conspiracy of silence. We may then add to the image of the three monkeys who see no evil, hear no evil, and speak no evil yet a fourth who might break the conspiracy any minute by breaching any of those taboos. Satirically expanding this trio to include a fourth member who is on the phone with one of America's leading investigative journalists, the following post-Watergate cartoon[1] captures the social forces that potentially undermine any conspiracy of silence and reminds us that our strong need to deny certain things is often counterbalanced by our equally strong desire to expose them.[2]

"Hello? Jack Anderson?"

© *The New Yorker Collection 1976 Arnie Levin from Cartoonbank.com. All rights reserved.*

From Awareness to Acknowledgement

Breaking a conspiracy of silence involves acknowledging the presence of the elephant in the room. Such acknowledgement (the absence of which, after all, is what distinctly characterizes open secrets) must take place in public. Acknowledging the elephant's presence in private is unlikely to end a conspiracy of silence involving more than two participants.

In marked contrast to the way in which the invention of the clothes dryer, for example, helped people conceal from the public the intimate trappings of their private lives,[3] breaking the silence thus thrusts what has always been private into the public eye. After all, while many Soviet citizens, for example, must have been quite aware of the atrocities committed under Stalin, it was not until his formal denunciation by Nikita Khrushchev, followed by the publication of Aleksandr Solzhenitsyn's harrowing account of the Gulag system in *One Day in the Life of Ivan Denisovich*, that the deafening silence surrounding them was *publicly* broken. By the same token, although many Israelis had known for nearly 40 years about the significant role played by Israel in the creation of the Palestinian refugee problem, it was the way in which Israeli historian Benny Morris breached their tacit agreement throughout those years not to discuss it in public that made his book *The Birth of the Palestinian Refugee Problem, 1947–1949* so controversial. And while millions of Americans must have been personally aware of George W. Bush's poor judgment, callousness, and remarkable lack of accountability in the aftermath of the 2003 invasion of Iraq, it was not until the flooding of the city of New Orleans following Hurricane Katrina in 2005 that the silence surrounding those rather blatant features of his presidency was publicly broken by the American media.[4]

Breaking a conspiracy of silence, in short, involves making the elephant's presence part of the public discourse. No wonder we use an image of a monkey whose mouth is covered to represent one of the key elements in any such conspiracy. An uncovered, and thus potentially open, mouth implies publicity, which is quintessentially antithetical to silence. As Bill Maher, the consummate silence breaker best known for his self-proclaimed "politically incorrect" tactlessness, facetiously reminds prospective viewers as he removes a tape covering his

mouth in an ad for his television show *Real Time with Bill Maher,*
"Duct tape is for windows, not for mouths."

Not surprisingly, publicity plays a critical role in efforts to
prevent as well as counteract denial. Note, for example, the role
of open communication in breaking through the wall of denial
often surrounding child sexual abuse, the moral necessity of
keeping Holocaust survivors' testimonies in the public domain,
or the way family intervention helps reverse the dynamics of
denial typically underlying alcohol and other drug addicts' relations with their enablers (as suggested by the subtitle of Helena
Roche's book *The Addiction Process: From Enabling to Intervention*).[5] Consider also gay activists' efforts to "out" (that is, publicize the covert homosexuality of) prominent public figures
during the AIDS epidemic of the 1980s as well as Republican
opponents of gay marriage in 2004.[6] As implied in the subtitle
of Warren Johansson and William Percy's book *Outing: Shattering the Conspiracy of Silence*, those were essentially "conspiracies
of publicity" designed to force homosexual individuals out of
their closets and thus break through the public wall of denial
surrounding the wide though largely unacknowledged presence
of homosexuality in society.

Notice the difference between the acts of outing specific
individuals and exposing how widespread homosexuality is as a
social phenomenon. Like the difference between laws that require local authorities to publicize the identities of specific sex
offenders and social movements designed to raise our general
awareness of rape or child pornography, it underscores the fundamental distinction between the acts of whistleblowing and
silence breaking. After all, what *silence breakers* like Emile Zola
(whose open letter "*J'accuse*" broke the public silence surrounding the rather blatant anti-Semitic undertones of the Dreyfus
affair) or Rolf Hochhuth (whose 1963 play *The Deputy* broke
the long, deafening silence surrounding the Vatican's complic-

ity in the Holocaust)[7] do is altogether different from what *whistleblowers* like Daniel Ellsberg, Erin Brockovich, Anita Hill, or Richard Clarke do. Rather than ordinary secrets the very existence of which we were unaware, silence breakers "reveal" open "secrets" of which we are aware yet unwilling to publicly acknowledge. In specifically publicizing, as we shall now see, "background" rather than "backstage" information,[8] they thus specifically help uncover "elephants" rather than the "skeletons" a whistleblower might bring to light.

Unveiling the Elephant

Needless to say, in order for its presence to be acknowledged the elephant has to be actively noticed. This presupposes pulling it out of the "background" and turning it into a "figure" of explicit attention. Calling attention to what is being ignored therefore requires the active reversal of figure and ground. Breaking conspiracies of silence, in other words, implies foregrounding the elephant in the room.[9]

Foregrounding the elephant presupposes enhancing its visibility by both turning the proverbial spotlight on it and opening people's eyes so that they become aware of it, as when the Allies forced the reality of the Holocaust into Germans' awareness by publicly displaying photographs of Nazi atrocities.[10] Like an imagined monster under one's bed, "elephants" draw their power from the fact that they lurk in the shadows, and they lose it as soon as one turns on the light. It is no wonder we regard situations where one suddenly becomes aware of something as "eye-openers." As soon as Adam and Eve, for example, eat the fruits of the tree of knowledge, "the eyes of them both [a]re opened" and they instantly realize that they are naked, something they had evidently seen yet never been explicitly aware of before.[11] Yet denial entails not only seeing but also hearing no evil, and breaking conspiracies of silence therefore also involves making "elephants" more audible. (In a highly charged scene in the film *Downhill Racer*, sitting in Camilla Sparv's car as she chatters on and on while evading the fact that she never showed up for the vacation they had planned to take together, an exasperated Robert Redford thus suddenly starts honking the car's horn in a desperate attempt to call attention to her yet unacknowledged withdrawal from their troubled relationship.)

As radio host Suzan Debini describes what she actually does on her aptly named silence-breaking talk show *Speaking Honestly* on Israel Radio's Arabic channel, "there are subjects that one is forbidden to talk about in our society, Arab society . . . The thing to do was always to sweep problems under the rug and say, 'There are no problems,' so I lifted up the rug and all the problems came out."[12] Such outspokenness is further exemplified by the speech made by the ever-iconoclastic documentary filmmaker Michael Moore upon accepting his 2003 Oscar. At an otherwise highly scripted formal ceremony specifically marked by its organizers' well-publicized effort to pretend to ignore the fact that it was being held only a few days after the United States invasion of Iraq he said, "We like nonfiction [yet] we live in fictitious times. We live in a time where we have fictitious election results that elect a fictitious president. We live in a time where we have a man who's sending us to war for fictitious reasons. Whether it's the fiction of duct tape or fiction of orange alerts, we are against this war, Mr. Bush. Shame on you, Mr. Bush, shame on you."[13] Like whistleblowing, such elephant foregrounding is often done in writing, as evidenced by incest survivor memoirs, "alternative" newspapers specifically dedicated to raising public awareness of issues traditionally ignored by their conventional counterparts, self-consciously outspoken social manifestos such as *Our Bodies, Ourselves* or *The*

Trouble with Islam, novels that explore the rarely discussed lone-liness one often encounters in marital bedrooms, and socio-logical studies specifically aimed at drawing attention to conventionally ignored aspects of social life.[14]

Foregrounding "elephants" often involves naming the con-ventionally unnameable thereby making it more discussable, as exemplified by Betty Friedan's famous critique of the silence historically surrounding the reality of being a housewife (the opening chapter of which is titled "The Problem That Has No Name" and begins with the words "The problem lay buried, unspoken, for many years in the minds of American women"), or the special edition of *Nightline* where Ted Koppel basically read aloud the names of the hundreds of American casualties of the war in Iraq in an attempt to foreground its publicly back-grounded human cost. It also presupposes a certain straight-forwardness. Essentially reversing tactics that help promote denial such as using euphemisms and "beating around the bush," one breaks conspiracies of silence by "calling a spade a spade," as when CNN's Wolf Blitzer implicitly called into question the credibility of President Clinton's emphatic denial of even knowing "that woman, Miss Lewinsky" by asking him in a press conference quite bluntly if there was something he wanted to say to her.[15]

"Elephants" are also foregrounded artistically (as exempli-fied by protest songs and antiwar exhibits like the "Arlington West" mock cemeteries on the beaches of Santa Barbara and Santa Monica)[16] as well as through humor. Consider, for ex-ample, the following *Daily Show with Jon Stewart* skit, in which a 28-page section blanked out from a United States congres-sional report in a lame attempt to "unmention" Saudi Arabia's evident yet highly embarrassing role in the 9/11 attacks is sa-tirically portrayed by deadpan comedian Stephen Colbert as an artistic tour de force: "But look at the report. I mean really look at it. Notice the use of bold black lines, the definition of negative space . . . This piece asks us: 'What is a government report? Does it need to contain information?' It forces the reader into an agonizing reappraisal of our societal dependency upon facts, names, dates, places . . . I say 'Bravo, Bush Administration, for this remarkable report!'"[17] No wonder so much humor revolves around traditionally taboo subjects such as sex and bodily functions as well as around social groups (the disabled, ethnic minorities) otherwise protected by the norms of "politically correct" discourse. Indeed, under certain political conditions, it is actually the only mode of discourse through which "elephants" may be safely foregrounded. After all, even in Nazi Germany one could at least indirectly point out the glaring discrepancy between one's leaders' actual looks and the Aryan ideal of manhood they so vigorously championed through jokes suggesting, tongue in cheek, that the ideal German should be "as blond as Hitler, as tall as Goebbels, [and] as slim as Göring."[18]

Needless to say, however, it is not only individuals who break conspiracies of silence. Indeed, there are many social movements whose entire raison d'etre is to raise public awareness of otherwise backgrounded social problems. The public demonstrations held by the Mothers of the Plaza de Mayo to protest Argentina's "Dirty War" against its political dissidents in the late 1970s[19] were a classic example of such collective elephant foregrounding, as are Take Back the Night rallies aimed at raising public awareness of sexual violence against women and efforts made by various human rights organizations to call attention to the plight of traditionally ignored groups like sweatshop workers and refugees.

Blind Eyes and Deaf Ears

Like silence itself, breaking it is a collaborative endeavor that involves an entire social system.[20] The first person who mentions the elephant in the room only begins the process of acknowledging its presence and, as the father of the little boy in "The Emperor's New Clothes" helps remind us, someone else must then second him. Indeed, for a conspiracy of silence to actually end, there ultimately need to be no more conspirators left to keep it alive.

As we might expect, to counteract the group pressure to keep the silence one usually uses the weight of numbers in order to break it as well. As demonstrated by the effectiveness of family intervention teams in overcoming alcohol and other drug addicts' denial, "it is fairly easy to discount or dismiss the claims of one person . . . [I]t becomes harder when these claims are made by a chorus. A group carries the necessary weight to break through to reality."[21]

As we saw earlier, the situation of being in a minority and facing the majority's pressure to maintain a conspiracy of silence becomes more pronounced as the number of conspirators increases. However, as more people join the silence breaker, the dynamics of the situation may ultimately shift and reach a "tipping point"[22] where the increasing social pressure on the remaining conspirators to also acknowledge the elephant's presence eventually overrides the social pressure to keep denying it.

Before that can happen, however, those conspirators must be ready to hear the proverbial child's announcement that the emperor has no clothes. Yet as Enron's Sherron Watkins found out when she told chairman Kenneth Lay that their company's accounting methods were improper, she had evidently underestimated "the seriousness of the emperor-has-no-clothes phenomenon . . . I said he was naked, and when he turned to the ministers around him, they said . . . he was clothed."[23]

Indeed, as famously exemplified by the Trojans' reaction to Cassandra's and Laocoön's warnings about the Greeks' wooden horse, our most common response to those who try to open our eyes is to actually ignore them. By expanding our conspiracy of silence to also swallow up anyone who tries to break it, we thus refrain from conceding the acknowledgement of the presence of the foregrounded elephant and effectively push it back to the background.

Consider, for example, the following incident that took place during the 1968 Columbia University student riots when radical student leader Mark Rudd

> rose from his aisle seat and walked . . . to the front of St. Paul's Chapel . . . as Vice President David B. Truman prepared to [eulogize] Martin Luther King . . . [He] cut in front of the vice president and placed himself in front of the microphone . . . "Dr. Truman and President Kirk are committing a moral outrage against the memory of Dr. King," Rudd said quietly . . . How, he demanded, can [they] eulogize a man who died while trying to unionize sanitation workers when they have, for years, fought the unionization of the University's own black and Puerto Rican workers? . . . And how, Rudd asked, can Columbia laud a man who preached non-violent disobedience when it is disciplining its own students for peaceful protest? . . . He stepped down from the stage and walked . . . down the center aisle and out the main chapel door . . . Forty others followed him. Truman continued on his way to the microphone and delivered his eulogy *as if nothing had happened*.[24]

Indeed, that is precisely how "The Emperor's New Clothes" also ends. As the people watching the royal procession start shouting that he has no clothes, the emperor pretends not to hear them: "The emperor shivered, for he was certain that they were right; but he thought, 'I must bear it until the procession

is over.' And he walked even more proudly, and the two gentle-
men of the imperial bedchamber went on carrying the train that
wasn't there."[25] As one might expect, our ability to ignore silence breakers depends largely on how much power they have.
It would have been much harder, for example, to pretend not to
have heard Mark Rudd's announcement had it actually been
made by Columbia president Kirk instead. The less power one
has, the easier it is for others to publicly ignore him.

Consider also Thomas Vinterberg's film *The Celebration*,
whose main protagonist, Christian, suddenly announces at a
large family gathering in honor of his father Helge's sixtieth
birthday that when he and his sister Linda, who recently killed
herself, were young, they were both molested by him—a charge
later corroborated by Linda's suicide note. Yet when he ends his
announcement none of the guests acknowledge having heard
it, thereby reminding us that, after they are publicly exposed,
even "skeletons" eventually become "elephants" if they continue to be ignored.

Conspirators of silence may also try to actively divert attention away from silence breakers (as when Helge tells the wait-
ers to refill everyone's glasses and Christian's brother Michael
asks someone to play something "nice and easy" on the piano)
or ask everybody around to "move on" and not "dwell on" the
elephants they exposed (as exemplified by George W. Bush's
attempt to use the "This is no time to play the blame game"
argument to deflect public criticism following Hurricane
Katrina, as well as by the way Arnold Schwarzenegger's 2003
gubernatorial campaign crisis-managed the various disturbing
and well-publicized reports about his behavior towards women).
They often also question their credibility, and thereby implicitly the reality of those elephants (as when Christian's sister
Helene says that what he said was untrue and his mother Elsie
adds that he always had trouble separating fact from fiction),

as well as try to actually hush them. One particularly hostile review of Kathryn Harrison's *The Kiss* indeed ends with the words "Hush up."[26]

Like whistleblowers,[27] silence breakers are also ridiculed, vilified, and often ostracized. Aside from their immediate punitive function, such retaliatory tactics are also designed to intimidate anybody else who contemplates breaking the conspiracy of silence, which indeed prevents many potential silence breakers from actually doing so.

Yet actual as well as potential silence breakers are not the only targets of such intimidation. So, in fact, is anybody who pays attention to them. After all, only when we all keep our mouths as well as our eyes and ears tightly shut will the proverbial elephant actually stay in the room.

chapter Six

Some Things Are
Better Left Unsaid

[Group members] keep a silence about things whose open discus-
sion would threaten the group's [sense of] solidarity . . . To break
such a silence is considered an attack against the group, a sort of
treason.

—Everett C. Hughes, "Good People and Dirty Work"

G iven the way we actually respond when someone breaks a
silence, no wonder the man who tells the king in the original version of "The Emperor's New Clothes" that "either I am
blind or you are naked" is in fact portrayed there as somebody
who had basically "nothing to lose."[1] After all, the deep resentment faced by whistleblowers who reveal ordinary secrets
(which is why many of them indeed prefer to remain anonymous) is typically also encountered by silence breakers who
expose open ones.

Despite their role as epistemic innovators who essentially
"open our eyes" and help us see things more clearly,[2] silence

breakers are by and large resented. While we may thoroughly enjoy reading about a fictional child who quite courageously helps his fellow countrymen see that their vain ruler actually wears no clothes, we generally respond quite differently to real-life individuals who try to break conspiracies of silence in which we happen to participate. Indeed, other than when the denial is widely regarded as a problem (as in the case of drug abuse) or when the breaking of the silence is done somewhat playfully (such as in a comedy show), silence breakers often generate deep resentment.

Saving Face

Part of the reason we resent silence breakers is that by defying the conventional figure-ground configurations that most of us take for granted, they disturb our cognitive tranquility. Even more importantly, they try to force us to acknowledge things we specifically choose to ignore to avoid getting hurt or upset. As one reviewer of Harrison's eye-opening memoir about incest has shrewdly noted, "Oedipus, we should remember, tore out his eyes as a punishment for his sin. Harrison chose to keep her eyes open. There are some who prefer blindness, the illusory innocence of those who have not paid, as she has, the heavy price of the awareness of sin. And *they are not ready to forgive her for having forced them to open their eyes as well.*"[3] People often get upset when confronted with information challenging their self-delusional view of the world around them. Many, indeed, prefer such delusions to painful realities and thus cherish one's "right to be an ostrich." Effectively contending that "ignorance is bliss" and that, to paraphrase John Lennon, living is easier with eyes closed, they essentially claim that "what you don't know won't hurt you."[4]

Yet denial also helps protect others besides oneself. Being unaware that the person with whom I am talking is constantly yawning may indeed be self-protective, yet pretending not to notice it so as not to embarrass *him* is clearly motivated by altruistic concerns.[5]

Not surprisingly, it is a small child who has not yet internalized the social norms of tactful inattention and discretion that help make "elephants" invisible and undiscussable who actually announces that the emperor has no clothes.[6] After all, doing so shows absolutely no concern for the emperor's feelings as well as sense of dignity. As such, it sharply contrasts with the empathic, considerate regard for others displayed, for example, by CNN's Bernard Shaw, who at the 2000 United States vice-presidential debate tactfully directed his question about the constitutional rights of gays and lesbians to Joe Lieberman rather than to Dick Cheney, whose own daughter is a lesbian. Indeed, though arguably somewhat hypocritical, the angry public backlash against the way John Kerry did call attention to that widely rumored yet rarely publicly mentioned elephant at the last 2004 presidential debate was indicative of the resentment often encountered by those who, in effectively disrupting widely established conspiracies of silence, seem to convey disregard for others' feelings and sense of dignity.[7] (By actually making the elephant's presence so blatantly obvious they also make it harder for the other conspirators to keep pretending not to notice it. After all, it is much easier to feign ignorance of something when no one turns the public spotlight on it.)

Being tactfully inattentive and discreet helps save others' face and avoids hurting their feelings. By pretending not to notice (and thereby preventing them from realizing that we actually did notice), for example, how much weight they have gained, the intestinal gases they release, or the fact that they constantly mispronounce our name, we are helping them avoid losing face.[8]

After all, commenting on one's stutter, bad breath, or hair loss can only hurt one's feelings and sense of dignity.

The notion that "some things are better left unsaid" also underscores the role of silence in preventing conflict.[9] A remarkably effective social lubricant, it helps minimize friction and thus makes social interaction more "smooth." No relationship could ever survive total straightforwardness, and the more delicate it is, the more important it is to make sure that certain matters are indeed never brought up.

Don't Rock the Boat

Yet it is not only individuals' but also groups' collective face that conspiracies of silence are designed to protect, and silence breakers are therefore usually viewed as more than just tactless. Indeed, they are often explicitly denounced by their fellow group members as traitors.[10]

It was the sight of "so much dirty linen about quotidian Jewish-American life hung out to dry on very public lines" that evidently bothered many Jewish critics of Philip Roth's early work. By the same token, it was probably not Jeffrey Masson's actual claims regarding Freud's alleged suppression of his own early view of child sexual abuse that so infuriated fellow psychoanalysts as much as the fact that he made them public. As likewise evident from many Muslims' and African-Americans' angry reactions to Irshad Manji's book *The Trouble with Islam: A Muslim's Call for Reform in Her Faith* and Bill Cosby's equally provocative public rebuke of black youth culture, washing one's group's "dirty linen" is particularly offensive to fellow group members when it is done in front of nonmembers. As *Time* magazine senior editor Christopher Farley bluntly put it, "there are . . . certain things . . . black people won't talk about in front of . . . white people . . . Bill Cosby *broke the unwritten rule of keeping black dirty laundry in black washing machines* . . . [A] number of my friends and relatives . . . were more horrified that he had gone public, not at the opinions themselves." (As if to underscore the fundamental yet commonly overlooked difference between silence breaking and whistleblowing, Cosby later responded by reminding Farley that it was not as if he had actually "divulged some secret about which no one knew . . . [W]here is the secret? The secret walks and it talks. From the hallways of the school to the street to the corner store and onto to public transportation, the dirty laundry *is* out there.")[11]

Not only can breaking a conspiracy of silence hurt a group's public image, it can also destroy its very fabric. As the rather suggestive common expression "don't rock the boat" seems to imply, it may disrupt the group's current political status quo thereby generating social instability.[12] A kingdom, after all, needs a king, even a naked one. No wonder it is often less powerful group members, who therefore have less to lose from such "turbulence," who are also the ones least threatened by silence breakers. The more powerful (and therefore having a greater stake in maintaining the current status quo) one is, the more likely one is to resent such boat-rocking "troublemakers."

Needless to say, calling attention to what other group members make a special effort to avoid is an implicitly subversive act. If sex, for example, claims Foucault, is "condemned to . . . silence, then the mere fact that one is speaking about it [is] a deliberate transgression . . . [When we speak about it] we are conscious of defying established power, our tone of voice shows that we know we are being subversive."[13] Indeed, as the poet Czesław Miłosz noted in his Nobel Prize acceptance speech, "in a room where people unanimously maintain a conspiracy of silence, one word of truth sounds like a pistol shot."[14] To break such a conspiracy is to breach some implicit social contract, and groups indeed treat those who violate their norms of attention and discourse just as they do any other social deviants who defy their authority and disregard their rules.

Many groups, in fact, view silence breakers as threats to their very existence. In the name of protecting their family, a woman who suspects that her husband is molesting their daughter may thus pretend not to notice it. As Sandra Butler, author of *Conspiracy of Silence: The Trauma of Incest*, has shrewdly observed, "keeping silent about the abuse, virtually denying its existence, is the only way [such a] family believes it can remain intact."[15]

Indeed, many families seem to feel much more threatened by efforts to call attention to instances of incest within them than by the offense itself, "the taboo against talking about it [thus being] stronger even than the taboo against doing it."[16] So, in fact, do many organizations when facing similar attempts to call attention to instances of corruption within them. By the same token, as Sonja, the naive German high-school student in the film *The Nasty Girl* who researches the imagined heroism of her townsfolk in an effort to highlight their "resistance" against the Nazi regime slowly realizes, they actually regard that shameful chapter in their town's history as much less disturbing than her inadvertent effort to unveil it. In fact, we often view conspiracies of silence as far less threatening than the efforts to end them.

chapter Seven

The Trouble
with Elephants

*Much unhappiness has come into the world because of . . . things
left unsaid.*

—Attributed to Fyodor Dostoyevsky

Having considered the benefits of conspiracies of silence,
let us now turn to examine their costs. Despite the considerable advantages they evidently offer individuals as well as
social groups, they also create serious problems for both.

Calculating what we ultimately gain and lose by opting to
see, hear, and speak no evil is largely a matter of weighing short-
term against long-term effects. Many of the advantages offered
by such conspiracies are but the short-term seeds of the long-
term problems they so often create. As Nancy Raine, author of
After Silence: Rape and My Journey Back, reflects on the years following her rape, "my continued silence was *a wounding disguised
as a healing*."[1] Indeed, much of what seems to benefit us in the
short run often comes to haunt us in the long run.

Inherently delusional, denial inevitably distorts one's sense of reality, a problem further exacerbated when others collude in it through their silence. After all, it is hard to remain convinced that one is actually seeing and not just imagining the elephant in the room when no one else seems to acknowledge its presence. Thus, in *The Kiss*, the fact that Harrison and her father never even mention to each other the rather blatant pass he made at her only increases her doubt whether he actually made it: "I think about the kiss all the time, but each time I consider asking my father about it, I find I can't open my mouth," partly as a result of which "I sometimes wonder if anything happened at all. I ask myself if I haven't perhaps made the whole thing up."[2] Her own denial is also further deepened by her boyfriend's: "'I made a mistake,' I tell my boyfriend. 'I exaggerated. I described it wrong. It wasn't exactly like that. He may have done it by accident' . . . My boyfriend, threatened himself by what I revealed, colludes with me in this process. *Together we forget . . .* what my father did."[3]

Uncorroborated personal experience is particularly unsettling for young children, who still rely on others to make sense of what they experience, like the five-year-old boy whose mother denies the very existence of her secret lover with whom the two only recently spent several hours.[4] When no one else around her ever mentions her father's rather obvious drinking problem, a child may thus come to "wonder if other people really see the elephant or if perhaps she made it up," and "since she can't ask anyone about the elephant, she just keeps on wondering."[5] The following nursery rhyme seems to capture the eerie feeling often generated by such uncorroborated experience:

Yesterday upon the stair
I saw a man who wasn't there
He wasn't there again today
Oh how I wish he'd go away.[6]

Lacking a firm basis for authenticating one's perceptual experience, one may thus come to distrust one's own senses and, as so chillingly portrayed in the film *Gaslight*, slowly lose one's grip on reality. The fact that no one else around us acknowledges the presence of "elephants" also tends to make them seem more frightening. Indeed, silence is not just a product, but also a major source, of fear (which also explains why it impedes the recovery of persons who have been traumatized).[7] To overcome fear we therefore often need to discuss the undiscussables that help produce it in the first place.[8]

As so poignantly portrayed in "The Emperor's New Clothes," conspiracies of silence always involve some dissonance between what one inwardly experiences and what one outwardly expresses: "'What!' thought the emperor. 'I can't see a thing!' [But] aloud he said, 'It is very lovely' . . . All the councilors, ministers, and men of great importance . . . saw no more than the emperor had seen [but] they said the same thing that he had said . . . 'It is magnificent! Beautiful! Excellent!' *All of their mouths agreed, though none of their eyes had seen anything.*"[9] As one can tell from these bitingly satirical descriptions, such dissonance involves the kind of duplicity associated by Orwell in *Nineteen Eighty-Four* with "doublethink": "His mind slid away into the labyrinthine world of doublethink. To know and not to know, to be conscious of complete truthfulness while telling carefully constructed lies, to hold simultaneously two opinions . . . knowing them to be contradictory."[10] Such duplicity presupposes a certain amount of cynicism. As a former Nazi doctor explains the inherently perverse logic of doublethink, "I couldn't ask [Dr.] Klein 'Don't send this man to the gas chamber,' because I didn't know that he went to the gas chamber. You see, that was a secret. Everybody [knew] the secret, but it was a secret." It also requires, however, a certain denial of one's feelings. Although those Nazi doctors certainly knew that Jews "were not being resettled but killed, and that the 'Final Solution' meant killing all of them," the fact that they could use such inherently anesthetic euphemistic expressions nevertheless meant that "killing . . . need[ed] not be experienced . . . as killing," and the more they used such language, the deeper they entered the "realm [of] nonfeeling," increasingly becoming emotionally numb.[11]

Needless to say, such denial of one's feelings is psychologically exhausting. "Don't think about it," Harrison tells herself as she tries to ignore her feelings about her incestuous relationship with her father; yet denying those feelings, she slowly comes to realize, "seems to require an enormous effort."[12]

Conspiracies of silence may also trigger feelings of loneliness. The discrepancy between what one actually notices and what others around one acknowledge noticing undermines the quest for intersubjectivity, the very essence of sociality,[13] and often generates a deep sense of isolation. Whereas open communication brings us closer, silence makes us feel more distant from one another. "The word, even the most contradictious word," notes Thomas Mann, "preserves contact —it is silence which isolates."[14] As a grieving poet desperately pleads,

> Oh, please, say her name.
> Oh, please, say "Barbara" again.
> Oh, please, let's talk about the elephant in the room.
> ....
> Can I say "Barbara" to you and not have you look away?
> For if I cannot, then you are leaving me
> Alone . . . In the room . . .
> With an elephant.[15]

By the same token, despite the fact that "so many of the clergy are gay," recalls a former gay seminarian, "it was never talked about or acknowledged . . . so I felt myself one of a kind and lived in a private hell." The same dynamic plays out amongst the unfulfilled housewives featured in Betty Friedan's *The Feminine Mystique* who were "so ashamed to admit [their] dissatisfaction that [they] never knew how many other women shared it."[16]

The intense feelings of loneliness often experienced by incest and rape victims are largely a product of such conspiracies of silence.[17] Thus, in *The Prince of Tides*, the trauma of being raped is further compounded for Tom, his mother, and his sister Savannah by the profound sense of isolation they feel as a result of their self-imposed silence: "I do not think the rape affected me as profoundly as my adherence to those laws of concealment and secrecy my mother had put into effect . . . We didn't even speak about it to one another. It was a private . . . covenant entered into by a country family remarkable for its stupidity and the protocols of denial it brought to disaster. In silence we would honor our private shame and make it unspeakable. Only Savannah broke the agreement . . . Three days later, she cut her wrists for the first time."[18] That certainly underscores the curative benefits offered by group settings that encourage trauma survivors to share their painful experiences with others in an effort to offset their feelings of isolation.[19]

Yet conspiracies of silence create problems not only for individuals. Indeed, many of those problems are unmistakably social.

As one might expect, ignoring an "elephant" takes a lot of concerted effort. After all, open secrets "are rarely secret. *Large amounts of* [social] *energy are consumed in our efforts to avoid noticing or speaking about them* ... When a family has [such a] secret, it is as if a ten-ton boulder were in the middle of the living room with no one being allowed to mention it. One always must walk around it; the chairs have to be placed differently; sidelong glances [may be cast in its direction] but not direct gazes. A series of conversational topics increasingly becomes forbidden."[20] As the common image of walking on eggshells so suggestively implies, such a room feels more like a minefield, as we "gingerly skirt the perimeter" of every topic of conversation, quite "aware that at any moment we might step on a land mine."[21]

Such conversations, of course, essentially revolve around anything but the elephant:

> We talk about the weather.
> We talk about work.
> We talk about everything else—
> Except the elephant in the room.[22]

We thus end up talking about "unimportant but discussable" matters and telling trivial stories essentially designed to cover up untold ones. To make sure that we do not actually acknowledge the elephant's presence by accidentally bumping into it we also keep a safe distance away from it by discussing only "safe" topics and avoiding ones from which we might inadvertently slip into undiscussable territory. As one might expect, our conversations thus touch on an increasingly smaller range of topics and we may gradually come to inhabit a labyrinthine social maze of closed doors and ever-narrower passages.[23]

Needless to say, co-ignoring the elephant in the room requires a major collaborative effort on everyone's part and is therefore socially exhausting. Not surprisingly, it can also generate a lot of tension. Indeed, the deeper the silence, the thicker the tension that builds around it.

Their concerted efforts to ignore the elephant may ultimately permeate every aspect of the relations among co-conspirators of silence. Indeed, their entire relationship may actually be "warped by this [elephant] to a large extent [because] it cannot be acknowledged or alluded to." As one incest survivor describes her family life, "our secret lived between us. It tainted every sentence we spoke."[24]

Thus, ironically, partly in an effort to preserve group solidarity, conspiracies of silence often undermine that very solidarity by impeding the development of honest, trusting relations that presuppose open communication.[25] Indeed, in an attempt to "protect" groups, they often make them become somewhat dysfunctional.

Silence is also morally corrosive, as it inevitably opens the door to abuse. No wonder it is, along with secrecy, one of wrongdoers' main weapons. Both cruelty and corruption, after all, "thriv[e] in the dark. To make [them] go away one needs to shine on [them] the brightest possible light."[26]

Silence, as the saying goes, is consent. By remaining silent about improper behavior we help normalize it, essentially enhancing its perpetuation by implicitly encouraging potential offenders to regard it as morally acceptable. A woman who pretends not to notice that her husband is molesting her daughter thus enables the abuse by essentially conveying her tacit approval.[27] By watching their senior colleagues ignore improper relationships between professors and students, junior faculty are likewise implicitly socialized to condone such transgressions, as are young soldiers who watch their commanding officer openly violate the rules of military conduct with no one ever mentioning it.

That explains why one might choose to use the image of the simian trio that has conventionally come to personify this culture of denial to satirically denounce it in an anti-rape ad along with the following caption: "Always say rape in a hushed tone. Otherwise, someone might be offended . . . or embarrassed . . . or even put in jail. But maybe it's about time people spoke out—in a loud voice—about the unfair treatment of rape victims. If you feel that way, tell someone, like the people you vote for."[28] Along similar lines, consider also the following East German satirical poem from the 1960s:

> He who turns a deaf ear to his time,
> And is blind to events of the day
> And utters but little of all that he knows:
> He alone will survive to grow old.
> Doubtlessly, though, one condition remains:
> To live so,
> One must himself be carved of stone.[29]

Indeed, breaking the silence is actually considered by many "a moral act par excellence." As Martin Luther King once said, "the day we see the truth and cease to speak is the day we begin to die." In fact, we may one day come to remember the Holocaust "not so much for the number of [its] victims as for the magnitude of the silence" surrounding it.[30]

The Ostrich and the Elephant

As evident from our relentless efforts to avoid them, "elephants" are fundamentally problematic entities. Yet by avoiding them we do nothing to solve the problems they represent.[31] Indeed, we may actually make them even worse.

"Elephants" rarely go away just because we pretend not to notice them. Although "everyone hopes that if we refuse to acknowledge their existence, maybe . . . they will go away,"[32] even the proverbial ostrich that sticks its head in the sand does not really make problems disappear by simply wishing them away. Fundamentally delusional, denial may help keep us unaware of unpleasant things around us but it cannot ever actually make them go away, as so vividly portrayed in the following scene from an incest survivor's nightmare:

> I am in a resort cottage, on vacation with my whole family: my husband, my parents, my grandfather and his wife, my sister and her husband, my aunt and uncle. The cottage is one big bare room, with a shiny brown floor. There are many bathrooms opening off the main room. But none of the toilets work. Some have been taken out and replaced with wastebaskets. All the toilets and all the wastebaskets are full to the brim with shit. And everyone is acting very cheerful and happy, their voices high and false, pretending that everything in the cottage is just as it should be.[33]

By enabling such collective denial, conspiracies of silence prevent us from confronting, and consequently solving, our problems (and, as exemplified by many Holocaust survivor families, may also help pass them on to future generations).[34] Remaining silent about actual instances of incest, for example, only helps exacerbate the pathological family dynamics underlying them.[35] By publicly announcing that his own son died of AIDS-related complications and urging South Africans to "give publicity to HIV/AIDS and not hide it" by "talk[ing] openly about people who die of AIDS,"[36] Nelson Mandela thus echoes gay activists' early warning that "Silence = Death," reminding us that the public silence still surrounding the alarming prevalence of HIV among us only makes it even more lethal.

Ironically, it is precisely the effort to collectively deny their ubiquitous presence that makes "elephants" so big. As soon as we acknowledge it they almost magically begin to shrink. And only then, when we no longer collude to ignore it, can we finally get the proverbial elephant out of the room.

Notes

Chapter One

1. Don Juan Manuel, "What Happened to the King and the Tricksters Who Made Cloth," in John E. Keller and L. Clark Keating (trans.), *The Book of Count Lucanor and Patronio* (Lexington: University Press of Kentucky, 1977 [1335]), 130–33.
2. Hans Christian Andersen, "The Emperor's New Clothes," in *The Complete Fairy Tales and Stories* (Garden City, NY: Doubleday, 1974 [1836]), 79.
3. See, for example, Jan E. Lewis and Peter S. Onuf (eds.), *Sally Hemings and Thomas Jefferson: History, Memory, and Civic Culture* (Charlottesville: University Press of Virginia, 1999); Tom Farrey, "Defining Bravery in College Sports," October 7, 2003, http://espn.go.com/ncaa/s/2003/1006/1632030. html#pop3
4. Michael Taussig, *Defacement: Public Secrecy and the Labor of the Negative* (Stanford: Stanford University Press, 1999), 50–51; Paul Krugman, "Gotta Have Faith," *New York Times*, December 17, 2002, A35. See also Chris Argyris, "Skilled

Incompetence," *Harvard Business Review*, September–October 1986, 76; Kathleen D. Ryan and Daniel K. Oestreich, *Driving Fear Out of the Office: How To Overcome the Invisible Barriers to Quality, Productivity, and Innovation* (San Francisco: Jossey-Bass, 1991), 30, 185–97; Dan Bar-On, *The Indescribable and the Undiscussable: Reconstructing Human Discourse after Trauma* (Budapest: Central European University Press, 1999), 155–215; Helen Fremont, *After Long Silence: A Memoir* (New York: Delta Books, 1999), 8, 31; Mark Jordan, *The Silence of Sodom: Homosexuality in Modern Catholicism* (Chicago: University of Chicago Press, 2000), 86; Elizabeth W. Morrison and Frances J. Milliken, "Organizational Silence: A Barrier to Change and Development in a Pluralistic World," *Academy of Management Review* 25 (2000), 706; Stanley Cohen, *States of Denial: Knowing about Atrocities and Suffering* (Cambridge: Polity, 2001), 148, 258; Ruth Wajnryb, *The Silence: How Tragedy Shapes Talk* (Crows Nest, Australia: Allen & Unwin, 2001), 33–36, 51, 85, 93, 96, 106–22, 187, 207, 249.

5. On the tension between private knowledge and public discourse, see also Timur Kuran, *Private Truths, Public Lies: The Social Consequences of Preference Falsification* (Cambridge, MA: Harvard University Press, 1995), 157. On "silent witnessing," see also Cohen, *States of Denial*, 75.

6. See, for example, Philip Vellacott, *Sophocles and Oedipus: A Study of Oedipus Tyrannus with a New Translation* (Ann Arbor: University of Michigan Press, 1971), 224–25; Léon Wurmser, "Blinding the Eye of the Mind: Denial, Impulsive Action, and Split Identity," in E. L. Edelstein et al. (eds.), *Denial: A Clarification of Concepts and Research* (New York: Plenum, 1989), 180; John Steiner, "The Retreat from Truth to Omnipotence in Sophocles' Oedipus at Colonus," *In-*

ternational Review of Psycho-Analysis 17 (1990), 233; John Steiner, *Psychic Retreats: Pathological Organisations in Psychotic, Neurotic, and Borderline Patients* (London: Routledge, 1993), 129; Cohen, *States of Denial*, 21–50.

7. Eviatar Zerubavel, "The Elephant in the Room: Notes on the Social Organization of Denial," presented at the "Toward a Sociology of Culture and Cognition" conference, Rutgers University, November 1999; Eviatar Zerubavel, "The Elephant in the Room: Notes on the Social Organization of Denial," in Karen A. Cerulo (ed.), *Culture in Mind: Toward a Sociology of Culture and Cognition* (New York: Routledge, 2002), 21–27. See also Everett C. Hughes, "Good People and Dirty Work," in *The Sociological Eye: Selected Papers* (Chicago: Aldine, 1971 [1962]), 91; Daniel Goleman, *Vital Lies, Simple Truths: The Psychology of Self-Deception* (New York: Touchstone Books, 1986), 226–27; Morrison and Milliken, "Organizational Silence," 708, 714–16; Thomas D. Beamish, "Accumulating Trouble: Complex Organization, A Culture of Silence, and A Secret Spill," *Social Problems* 47 (2000), 485–86; Cohen, *States of Denial*, x; Craig C. Pinder and Karen P. Harlos, "Employee Silence: Quiescence and Acquiescence as Responses to Perceived Injustice," *Research in Personnel and Human Resources Management* 20 (2001), 331–69; Thomas D. Beamish, *Silent Spill: The Organization of an Industrial Crisis* (Cambridge, MA: MIT Press, 2002), 66–70; Eric Klinenberg, *Heat Wave: A Social Autopsy of Disaster in Chicago* (Chicago: University of Chicago Press, 2002), 36; Donald Cozzens, *Sacred Silence: Denial and the Crisis in the Church* (Collegeville, MN: The Liturgical Press, 2002), 24, 41; Kari M. Norgaard, "Denial, Privilege and Global Environmental Justice: The Case of Climate Change," presented at the annual meeting of the American Sociological

Association, Atlanta, 2003; Kari M. Norgaard, "People Want To Protect Themselves A Little Bit: Emotions, Denial and Social Movement Non-Participation—The Case of Global Climate Change," presented at the annual meeting of the American Sociological Association, Atlanta, 2003.

8. Kathryn Harrison, *The Kiss* (New York: Avon Books, 1997), 74, 137.

9. Sylvia Fraser, *My Father's House: A Memoir of Incest and of Healing* (New York: Perennial Library, 1989 [1987]), 21.

10. I. F. Stone, "It Pays To Be Ignorant," *New York Review of Books*, August 9, 1973, 8.

11. On the Japanese origin of these three monkeys, see Rudolph Brasch, *How Did It Begin? Customs and Superstitions and Their Romantic Origins* (Croydon, Australia: Longmans, Green & Co., 1965), 167–68; Wolfgang Mieder, "The Proverbial Three Wise Monkeys," *Midwestern Journal of Language and Folklore* 7 (1981), 8–9; Wolfgang Mieder, *Tradition and Innovation in Folk Literature* (Hanover, NH: University Press of New England, 1987), 161.

12. Morrison and Milliken, "Organizational Silence," 706.

13. Derrick Jensen, *A Language Older Than Words* (New York: Context Books, 2000), 4. See also Nancy V. Raine, *After Silence: Rape and My Journey Back* (New York: Crown, 1998), 120; Judith L. Herman, *Trauma and Recovery* (New York: BasicBooks, 1992), 1.

14. Nadine Fresco, "Remembering the Unknown," *International Review of Psycho-Analysis* 11 (1984), 418; Wajnryb, *The Silence*.

15. See, for example, Arlene Stein, "Trauma Stories, Identity Work, and the Politics of Recognition," in Judith M. Gerson and Diane L. Wolf (eds.), *De-ghettoizing the Holocaust: Collective Memory, Identity, and Trauma* (Durham, NC: Duke University Press, forthcoming).

16. See John Gross, "Intimations of Mortality," in D. J. Enright (ed.), *Fair of Speech: The Uses of Euphemism* (Oxford: Oxford University Press, 1985), 203–19; Keith Allan and Kate Burridge, *Euphemism and Dysphemism: Language Used as Shield and Weapon* (New York: Oxford University Press, 1991), 78–115; 153–67, 172–91.

17. Walter Laqueur, *The Terrible Secret: Suppression of the Truth about Hitler's "Final Solution"* (Boston: Little, Brown & Co., 1980), 142.

18. Bar-On, *The Indescribable and the Undiscussable*, 155; Michael Billig, *Freudian Repression: Conversation Creating the Unconscious* (Cambridge: Cambridge University Press, 1999), 52; Frances J. Milliken et al., "An Exploratory Study of Employee Silence: Issues that Employees Don't Communicate Upward and Why," *Journal of Management Studies* 40 (2003), 1453–76.

19. Laqueur, *The Terrible Secret*, 123–51; Raul Hilberg, *Perpetrators, Victims, Bystanders: The Jewish Catastrophe 1933–1945* (New York: HarperCollins, 1992), 195; Cohen, *States of Denial*, 148.

20. Louise Pound, "American Euphemisms for Dying, Death, and Burial," *American Speech* 11 (1936), 195–202; Jana Staton et al., *A Few Months to Live: Different Paths to Life's End* (Washington, DC: Georgetown University Press, 2001), 38–39, 54; Robert J. Lifton, "Imagining the Real," in Robert J. Lifton and Richard Falk (eds.), *Indefensible Weapons: The Political and Psychological Case against Nuclearism* (New York: Basic Books, 1982), 3–125; David S. Greenwald and Steven J. Zeitlin, *No Reason To Talk about It: Families Confront the Nuclear Taboo* (New York: W. W. Norton, 1987); Robert J. Lifton and Greg Mitchell, *Hiroshima in America: Fifty Years of Denial* (New York: G. P. Putnam's Sons, 1995). See also Barney G. Glaser

and Anselm L. Strauss, _Awareness of Dying_ (Chicago: University of Chicago Press, 1965); Jay Katz, _The Silent World of Doctor and Patient_ (New York: Free Press, 1984), 213–15.

21. Jordan, _The Silence of Sodom_, 165. See also Michel Foucault, _The History of Sexuality_ (New York: Pantheon, 1978 [1976]), vol. 1, 3–5, 17; Kathryn Harrison, _Thicker than Water_ (New York: Random House, 1991), 106; Elizabeth Stuart, _Chosen: Gay Catholic Priests Tell Their Stories_ (London: Geoffrey Chapman, 1993), 44; Cozzens, _Sacred Silence_, 125–31.

22. Lily Pincus and Christopher Dare, _Secrets in the Family_ (New York: Pantheon Books, 1978), 10–11.

23. Dan Bar-On, _Legacy of Silence: Encounters with Children of the Third Reich_ (Cambridge, MA: Harvard University Press, 1989), 328. See also 33, 168, 193, 243, 249, 254, 262, 273; Goleman, _Vital Lies, Simple Truths_, 227–28; Susan Griffin, _A Chorus of Stones: The Private Life of War_ (New York: Doubleday, 1992), 166; Ernestine Schlant, _The Language of Silence: West German Literature and the Holocaust_ (New York: Routledge, 1999); Vamik D. Volkan et al., _The Third Reich in the Unconscious: Transgenerational Transmission and Its Consequences_ (New York: Brunner-Routledge, 2002), 150–51.

24. For a classic sociological analysis of embarrassment, see Erving Goffman, "Embarrassment and Social Organization," _American Journal of Sociology_ 62 (1956), 264–74.

25. Nancy Nason-Clark, "Has the Silence Been Shattered or Does a Holy Hush Still Prevail?: Defining Violence against Women within Christian Churches," in Anson Shupe et al. (eds.), _Bad Pastors: Clergy Misconduct in Modern America_, (New York: New York University Press, 2000), 69–89; Atul Gawande, _Complications: A Surgeon's Notes on an Imperfect Science_ (New York: Picador, 2002), 88–106.

26. Marion H. Typpo and Jill M. Hastings, _An Elephant in the Living Room: A Leader's Guide for Helping Children of Alcoholics_

(Center City, MN: Hazelden, 1984), 15. See also i–ii, 69, 83, 113; Stephanie Brown, *Treating Adult Children of Alcoholics: A Developmental Perspective* (New York: John Wiley, 1988), 9, 27, 35, 72, 171.

27. Yitzhak Laor, "We Write You, Homeland," in *Narratives with No Natives: Essays on Israeli Literature* (Tel Aviv: Hotzaat Hakibbutz Hameuchad, 1995), 121, 163; Nicholas D. Kristof, "Are the Saudis the Enemy?" *New York Times*, October 22, 2002, A31; Kanan Makiya, *Cruelty and Silence: War, Tyranny, Uprising, and the Arab World* (New York: W. W. Norton, 1993); Rachel L. Swarns, "Mugabe's Aides Declare Him Winner of Zimbabwe Vote," *New York Times*, March 14, 2002, A3. See also Martin Amis, *Koba the Dread: Laughter and the Twenty Million* (New York: Hyperion, 2002), 170.

28. Adam Jaworski, *The Power of Silence: Social and Pragmatic Perspectives* (Newbury Park, CA: Sage, 1993), xii; Bernard P. Dauenhauer, *Silence: The Phenomenon and Its Ontological Significance* (Bloomington: Indiana University Press, 1980), 4; Wajnryb, *The Silence*, 25. See also William J. Samarin, "Language of Silence," *Practical Anthropology* 12 (1965), 115; Deborah Tannen and Muriel Saville-Troike (eds.), *Perspectives on Silence* (Norwood, NJ: Ablex, 1985); Jaworski, *The Power of Silence*, 81–82; King-Kok Cheung, *Articulate Silences: Hisaye Yamamoto, Maxine Hong Kingston, Joy Kogawa* (Ithaca, NY: Cornell University Press, 1993), 1; Peter Tiersma, "The Language of Silence," *Rutgers Law Review* 48 (1995), 1–99; Frederick B. Bird, *The Muted Conscience: Moral Silence and the Practice of Ethics in Business* (Westport, CT: Quorum Books, 1996), 34–48; Pinder and Harlos, "Employee Silence," 334; Linn Van Dyne et al., "Conceptualizing Employee Silence and Employee Voice as Multidimensional Constructs," *Journal of Management Studies* 40 (2003), 1365.

29. Wajnryb, *The Silence*, 165. See also 75, 143; Bar-On, *The Indescribable and the Undiscussable*, 165.

30. Wajnryb, *The Silence*, 31. See also Dag Hammarskjöld, *Markings* (New York: Alfred A. Knopf, 1964 [1963]), 78; Harrison, *Thicker than Water*, 244.

31. Leonid N. Andreyev, "Silence," in *The Little Angel and Other Stories* (Freeport, NY: Books for Libraries Press, 1971 [1910]), 130. See also 131–32, 140, 142, 144; Stephen Kern, *The Culture of Time and Space 1880–1918* (Cambridge, MA: Harvard University Press, 1983), 170.

32. Mica Pollock, *Colormute: Race Talk Dilemmas in an American School* (Princeton, NJ: Princeton University Press, 2004), 73, 79–82, 175, 184, 188, 193, 203–06, 217, 237.

33. Taussig, *Defacement*, 50; Herbert Fingarette, *Self-Deception* (London: Routledge & Kegan Paul, 1969), 47–48, 66. See also Shlomo Breznitz (ed.), *The Denial of Stress* (New York: International Universities Press, 1983), 100; Jamie L. Mullaney, "Like A Virgin: Temptation, Resistance, and the Construction of Identities Based on 'Not Doings,'" *Qualitative Sociology* 24 (2001), 10–13; Jamie L. Mullaney, *Everyone Is NOT Doing It: Abstinence and Personal Identity* (Chicago: University of Chicago Press, 2005), 3–7.

34. See also Włodzimierz Sobkowiak, "Silence and Markedness Theory," in Adam Jaworski (ed.), *Silence: Interdisciplinary Perspectives* (Berlin and New York: Mouton de Gruyter, 1997), 39–61; Cozzens, *Sacred Silence*, 11–12.

35. Chuck 45, "An Elephant in their Midst," October 9, 2000, www.thegully.com/essays/gaymundo/001009elephant.html

36. Typpo and Hastings, *An Elephant in the Living Room*, i.

37. Congressman John Spratt, featured on National Public Radio's *All Things Considered*, August 13, 2002.

38. Amis, *Koba the Dread*, 251. See also 170.

39. Bill Adair and Katherine Gazella, "It Lasted 72 Minutes Without a Mention," *St. Petersburg Times*, January 28, 1998,

8A; David Bauder, "For TV Networks, Big Coverage Day," *Associated Press Online*, January 19, 1999; Jennifer Harper, "Media Highlights Surreal Day with Trial, State of the Union," *Washington Times*, January 19, 1999, A11 [emphasis added]. See also Joan Ryan, "Guns in Society: The Real Problem," *San Francisco Chronicle*, August 22, 1999, 1, Z1.

40. See, for example, Norman L. Farberow, "Introduction," in *Taboo Topics* (New York: Atheling Books, 1966 [1963]), 2; Gordon W. Allport, "Foreword," In Norman L. Farberow (ed.), *Taboo Topics* (New York: Atheling Books, 1966 [1963]), v–vii; Wayne Brekhus, "A Sociology of the Unmarked: Redirecting Our Focus," *Sociological Theory* 16 (1998), 36.

41. See also Mullaney, *Everyone Is NOT Doing It*, 3–7, 25–29.

42. See, for example, Pollock, *Colormute*; Jordan, *The Silence of Sodom*; Greenwald and Zeitlin, *No Reason To Talk about It*; Wajnryb, *The Silence*.

43. See also Eviatar Zerubavel, "Generally Speaking: The Logic and Mechanics of Social Pattern Analysis," presented at the annual meeting of the American Sociological Association, San Francisco, August 2004.

44. Kuran, *Private Truths, Public Lies*, xi.

45. C. Fred Alford, *Whistleblowers: Broken Lives and Organizational Power* (Ithaca, NY: Cornell University Press, 2001), 21.

Chapter Two

1. See Jill M. Taylor et al., *Between Voice and Silence: Women and Girls, Race and Relationship* (Cambridge, MA: Harvard University Press, 1995), 99–106.

2. On such activities, see also Erving Goffman, *Behavior in Public Places: Notes on the Social Organization of Gatherings* (New York: Free Press, 1963), 43–53.

3. See Sigmund Freud, *The Psychopathology of Everyday Life* (New York: W. W. Norton, 1960 [1901], 53–105; Edward T. Hall, *The Hidden Dimension* (Garden City, NY: Doubleday, 1966), 113–64. See also Thomas S. Kuhn, *The Structure of Scientific Revolutions* (Chicago: University of Chicago Press, 1962), 111, 122; Eviatar Zerubavel, *Social Mindscapes: An Invitation to Cognitive Sociology* (Cambridge, MA: Harvard University Press, 1997), 45–46; Ruth Simpson, "The Germ Culture," presented at the annual meeting of the American Sociological Association, Chicago, 2002.

4. See also Christopher D. Stone, *Should Trees Have Standing?* (Los Altos, CA: William Kaufmann, 1974), 6–7.

5. Alice Mills and Jeremy Smith, "Introduction," in *Utter Silence: Voicing the Unspeakable* (New York: Peter Lang, 2001), 1.

6. See also Zerubavel, *Social Mindscapes*, 6–12.

7. Ibid., 33–34, 46–48. See also Frederic C. Bartlett, *Remembering: A Study in Experimental and Social Psychology* (Cambridge: Cambridge University Press, 1932), 254–55; Ludwik Fleck, *Genesis and Development of a Scientific Fact* (Chicago: University of Chicago Press, 1981 [1935], 38–51, 98–111.

8. See Asia Friedman, "Sex Seen: The Socio-Optical Construction of Sexed Bodies," presented at the annual meeting of the American Sociological Association, San Francisco, August 2004; Zerubavel, *Social Mindscapes*, 39; Erich Goode and Nachman Ben-Yehuda, *Moral Panics: The Social Construction of Deviance* (Oxford: Blackwell, 1994).

9. Eviatar Zerubavel, "Personal Information and Social Life," *Symbolic Interaction* 5, no. 1 (1982), 107. See also Herbert Fingarette, *Self-Deception* (London: Routledge & Kegan Paul, 1969), 44; Shoshana Felman and Dori Laub (eds.), *Testimony: Crises of Witnessing in Literature, Psychoanalysis, and History* (New York: Routledge, 1992), 83.

10. Zerubavel, *Social Mindscapes*, 32–33, 46–51.

11. Marion H. Typpo and Jill M. Hastings, *An Elephant in the Living Room: Leader's Guide for Helping Children of Alcoholics* (Center City, MN: Hazelden, 1984), i.

12. Georg Simmel, "The Field of Sociology," in Kurt H. Wolff (ed.), *The Sociology of Georg Simmel* (New York: Free Press, 1950 [1917]), 7–8; Fleck, *Genesis and Development of A Scientific Fact*; Kuhn, *The Structure of Scientific Revolutions*, 126; Eviatar Zerubavel, *Patterns of Time in Hospital Life: A Sociological Perspective* (Chicago: University of Chicago Press, 1979), xvi–xviii; Eviatar Zerubavel, "If Simmel Were a Fieldworker: On Formal Sociological Theory and Analytical Field Research," *Symbolic Interaction* 3, no.2 (1980), 25–33.

13. C. Wright Mills, *The Sociological Imagination* (London: Oxford University Press, 1959), 5–11; Zerubavel, *Social Mindscapes*, 1–22.

14. Ernest G. Schachtel, *Metamorphosis: On the Development of Affect, Perception, Attention, and Memory* (New York: Basic Books, 1959), 251–78; Arien Mack and Irvin Rock, *Inattentional Blindness* (Cambridge, MA: MIT Press, 1998.

15. John Hotchkiss, "Children and Conduct in a Ladino Community in Chiapas, Mexico," *American Anthropologist* 69 (1967), 711–18; Barbara Rogoff, *Apprenticeship in Thinking: Cognitive Development in Social Context* (New York: Oxford University Press, 1990), 124–26.

16. Zerubavel, *Social Mindscapes*, 50.

17. Joan P. Emerson, "Behavior in Private Places: Sustaining Definitions of Reality in Gynecological Examinations," in Hans-Peter Dreitzel (ed.), *Recent Sociology No. 2: Patterns of Communicative Behavior* (London: Macmillan, 1970), 78 [emphasis added].

18. Ibid., 83. See also 86.

19. Erving Goffman, _The Presentation of Self in Everyday Life_ (Garden City, NY: Doubleday Anchor, 1959), 151–53; Erving Goffman, "Footing," in _Forms of Talk_ (Philadelphia: University of Pennsylvania Press, 1981 [1979]), 131–37.

20. Goffman, "Footing," 132. See also Erving Goffman, "Fun in Games," in _Encounters: Two Studies in the Sociology of Interaction_ (Indianapolis: Bobbs-Merrill, 1961), 63–64; Erving Goffman, _Frame Analysis: An Essay on the Organization of Experience_ (New York: Harper Colophon, 1974), 225.

21. See also Murray S. Davis, _Smut: Erotic Reality / Obscene Ideology_ (Chicago: University of Chicago Press, 1983), 134–39, 144–50, 157–59; Eviatar Zerubavel, _The Fine Line: Making Distinctions in Everyday Life_ (Chicago: University of Chicago Press, 1993 [1991]), 40–41, 44; Wayne Brekhus, "Social Marking and the Mental Coloring of Identity: Sexual Identity Construction and Maintenance in the United States," _Sociological Forum_ 11 (1996), 497–522.

22. Goffman, "Fun in Games," 19–26; Goffman, _Frame Analysis_, 201–46.

23. See also Kristen Purcell, "In a League of Their Own: Mental Leveling and the Creation of Social Comparability in Sport," _Sociological Forum_ 11 (1996), 435–56.

24. Zygmunt Bauman, _Modernity and the Holocaust_ (Ithaca, NY: Cornell University Press, 2000 [1989]), 100–101; Zerubavel, _The Fine Line_, 59.

25. Alexander Mitscherlich and Margarete Mitscherlich, _The Inability to Mourn: Principles of Collective Behavior_ (New York: Grove Press, 1975 [1967]), 91; Genesis 2:16–17.

26. Zerubavel, _Social Mindscapes_, 32.

27. Emile Durkheim, _The Elementary Forms of Religious Life_ (New York: Free Press, 1995 [1912]), 308–9.

28. Ibid., 309–10.

29. Thomas D. Beamish, *Silent Spill: The Organization of an Industrial Crisis* (Cambridge, MA: MIT Press, 2002), 66–70; Patricia Y. Martin and Robert A. Hummer, "Fraternities and Rape on Campus," *Gender and Society* 3 (1989), 463–64; Dominic Casciani, "How the Media Covered Up the Scandal," *BBC News* (World Edition), January 30, 2003, http://news.bbc.co.uk/2/hi/uk_news/2707571.stm; "Mrs. Simpson Had Secret Lover," CNN.com, January 30, 2003, www.cnn.com/2003/WORLD/europe/01/29/edward.files/ See also David Caute, *The Espionage of the Saints: Two Essays on Silence and the State* (London: Hamish Hamilton, 1986), ix; Stanley Cohen, *States of Denial: Knowing about Atrocities and Suffering* (Cambridge: Polity, 2001), 66.

30. Ruth Wajnryb, *The Silence: How Tragedy Shapes Talk* (Crows Nest, Australia: Allen & Unwin, 2001), 246.

31. Mark Jordan, *The Silence of Sodom: Homosexuality in Modern Catholicism* (Chicago: University of Chicago Press, 2000), 16.

32. George Orwell, *Nineteen Eighty-Four* (New York: New American Library, 1961 [1949]), 252.

33. Michel Foucault, *The History of Sexuality* (New York: Pantheon, 1978 [1976]), vol. 1, 17. See also 3–5.

34. Robert J. Lifton, *The Nazi Doctors: Medical Killing and the Psychology of Genocide* (New York: Basic Books, 1986), 445–46. See also Robert J. Lifton, "Imagining the Real," in Robert J. Lifton and Richard Falk (eds.), *Indefensible Weapons: The Political and Psychological Case against Nuclearism* (New York: Basic Books, 1982), 107.

35. Robert M. Adams, "Soft Soap and the Nitty-Gritty," in D. J. Enright (ed.), *Fair of Speech: The Uses of Euphemism* (Oxford: Oxford University Press, 1985), 48.

36. Penelope Brown and Stephen C. Levinson, *Politeness: Some Universals in Language Use* (Cambridge: Cambridge University Press, 1987 [1978]), 70.

37. See also Barney G. Glaser and Anselm L. Strauss, *Awareness of Dying* (Chicago: University of Chicago Press, 1965), 39, 67–68, 78; Judith Martin, *Miss Manners' Guide for the Turn-of-the-Millennium* (New York: Fireside, 1990), 95–99.
38. Martin, *Miss Manners' Guide for the Turn-of-the-Millennium*, 100. See also 94–95, 106–13, 562–63; Erving Goffman, *The Presentation of Self in Everyday Life*, 229.
39. Rachelle Germana, "Domestic Violence: A Cognitive Approach" (Rutgers University, Department of Sociology, 2002).
40. Goffman, *Behavior in Public Places*, 84–87. See also Goffman, *The Presentation of Self in Everyday Life*, 230; Goffman, "Fun in Games," 63.
41. Lily Pincus and Christopher Dare, *Secrets in the Family* (New York: Pantheon Books, 1978), 145. See also Martin, *Miss Manners' Guide for the Turn-of-the-Millennium*, 147.
42. Hans-Georg Gadamer, *Truth and Method* (New York: Crossroad, 1975 [1960]), 16–17.
43. See also Barry Schwartz, "Vengeance and Forgiveness: The Uses of Beneficence in Social Control," *School Review* 86 (1978), 655–68; Charles L. Bosk, *Forgive and Remember: Managing Medical Failure* (Chicago: University of Chicago Press, 1979), 177–81; Frederick B. Bird, *The Muted Conscience: Moral Silence and the Practice of Ethics in Business* (Westport, CT: Quorum Books, 1996), 120–21; Eviatar Zerubavel, *Time Maps: Collective Memory and the Social Shape of the Past* (Chicago: University of Chicago Press, 2003), 93–95.
44. Goffman, "Fun in Games," 56; Goffman, *Behavior in Public Places*, 84; François Truffaut, *Stolen Kisses*. See also Martin S. Weinberg, "Sexual Modesty, Social Meanings, and the Nudist Camp," *Social Problems* 12 (1965), 311–18.
45. Goffman, "Fun in Games," 55; Goffman, *The Presentation of Self in Everyday Life*, 231. See also Erving Goffman, "On

Face Work: An Analysis of Ritual Elements in Social Inter-action," in *Interaction Ritual: Essays on Face-to-Face Behavior* (Garden City, NY: Doubleday Anchor, 1967 [1955]), 18.

46. Mica Pollock, *Colormute: Race Talk Dilemmas in an American School* (Princeton, NJ: Princeton University Press, 2004).

47. Robin E. Sheriff, "Exposing Silence as Cultural Censor-ship: A Brazilian Case," *American Anthropologist* 102 (2000), 114–32.

Chapter Three

1. Luigi Pirandello, *Tonight We Improvise* (New York: Samuel French, 1960 [1932]).

2. For a more extensive discussion of such attempts, see Eviatar Zerubavel, *The Fine Line: Making Distinctions in Everyday Life* (Chicago: University of Chicago Press, 1993 [1991]), 108–12.

3. Johanna Foster, "Condom Negotiation and the Politics of Relevance" (Rutgers University, Department of Sociology, 1995).

4. See also Robin E. Sheriff, "Exposing Silence as Cultural Censorship: A Brazilian Case," *American Anthropologist* 102 (2000), 114.

5. I. F. Stone, "It Pays To Be Ignorant," *New York Review of Books*, August 9, 1973, 6–8. See also Stanley Cohen, *States of Denial: Knowing about Atrocities and Suffering* (Cambridge: Pol-ity, 2001), 68; Dan Ryan, "Getting the Word Out: Notes on the Social Organization of Notification," *Sociological Theory*, forthcoming.

6. On the "cognitive division of labor" within social systems, see also Eviatar Zerubavel, *Social Mindscapes: An Invitation to*

Cognitive Sociology (Cambridge, MA: Harvard University Press, 1997), 18–19.

7. See also Ruth Wajnryb, *The Silence: How Tragedy Shapes Talk* (Crows Nest, Australia: Allen & Unwin, 2001), 6.

8. Elisabeth Bumiller and Patrick E. Tyler, "Putin Questions U.S. Terror Allies," *New York Times*, November 23, 2002, A1.

9. Michael Moore, "A Letter to George W. Bush on the Eve of War," *AlterNet.Org*, March 17, 2003, http://72.14.207.104/search?q=cache:T-1hmuwkCmUJ;www.alternet.org/story.html%3FStoryID%3D15406+%22A+Letter+to+George+W.+Bush+on+the+Eve+of+War%22&hl=en; Dan Pletch, "Weapons of Mass Distraction: President Bush Wouldn't Want to Talk about the Many Issues which the Iraq Crisis Is Obscuring," *Observer Worldview*, September 29, 2002, www.observer.co.uk/worldview/story/0,11581,800486,00.html; Maureen Dowd, "Yo, Ayatollahs!" *New York Times*, May 25, 2003, section 4, 9. See also François Truffaut, *Hitchcock* (New York: Touchstone, 1985 [1983]), 138–39.

10. See also Zerubavel, *Social Mindscapes*, 97; Eviatar Zerubavel, *Time Maps: Collective Memory and the Social Shape of the Past* (Chicago: University of Chicago Press, 2003), 4.

11. Bernard C. Cohen, *The Press and Foreign Policy* (Princeton: Princeton University Press, 1963), 13 [emphasis added]. See also Timur Kuran, *Private Truths, Public Lies: The Social Consequences of Preference Falsification* (Cambridge, MA: Harvard University Press, 1995), 187.

12. See, for example, Maxwell E. McCombs and Donald L. Shaw, "The Agenda-Setting Function of Mass Media," *Public Opinion Quarterly* 36 (1972), 176–87; Herbert J. Gans, *Deciding What's News: A Study of CBS Evening News, NBC Nightly News, Newsweek, and Time* (New York: Random House, 1979); Eric Klinenberg, *Heat Wave: A Social Autopsy*

of Disaster in Chicago (Chicago: University of Chicago Press, 2002), 190–224.

13. See, for example, Joshua Meyrowitz, "The Press Rejects a Candidate," *Columbia Journalism Review*, March/April 1992, 46–47.

14. Mark Fishman, "Crime Waves as Ideology," *Social Problems* 25 (1978), 531–43. See also Anthony Downs, "Up and Down with Ecology: The 'Issue-Attention Cycle,'" *The Public Interest* 28 (1972), 38–39.

15. Arthur L. Stinchcombe, *Constructing Social Theories* (New York: Harcourt, Brace & World, 1968), 243; Zerubavel, *Time Maps*, 106.

16. Zerubavel, *Social Mindscapes*, 17. See also Thomas E. DeGloma, "Memory and the Cognitive Masking of Child Sex Abuse: Framing and Cognitive Asymmetries of Power in the Family," presented at the annual meeting of the American Sociological Association, Atlanta, August 2003.

17. Arthur Koestler, *The Act of Creation* (New York: Macmillan, 1964), 105–44, 230–33; Jonathan Miller, *The Body in Question* (New York: Random House, 1978); Mattei Dogan and Robert Pahre, *Creative Marginality: Innovation at the Intersections of the Social Sciences* (Boulder, CO: Westview, 1990); Zerubavel, *The Fine Line*, 117; Eviatar Zerubavel, "The Rigid, the Fuzzy, and the Flexible: Notes on the Mental Sculpting of Academic Identity," *Social Research* 62 (1995), 1097–98.

18. Stone, "It Pays To Be Ignorant," 7. See also Elaine Sciolino and Neil MacFarquhar, "Naming of Hijackers as Saudis May Further Erode Ties to U.S.," *New York Times*, October 25, 2001, B4.

19. Elmer Luchterhand, "Knowing and Not Knowing: Involvement in Nazi Genocide," in Paul Thompson (ed.), *Our Common History: The Transformation of Europe* (Atlantic Highlands, NJ: Humanities Press, 1982), 263; Claude Lanzmann,

Shoah: An Oral History of the Holocaust (New York: Pantheon, 1985), 26, 97; Gordon J. Horwitz, *In the Shadow of Death: Living Outside the Gates of Mauthausen* (New York: Free Press, 1990), 27, 32, 112, 175.

20. Michael Taussig, *Defacement: Public Secrecy and the Labor of the Negative* (Stanford: Stanford University Press, 1999), 6. See also 50.

21. David Bankier, *The Germans and the Final Solution: Public Opinion under Nazism* (Oxford: Blackwell, 1992), 104–15, 131–32; Luchterhand, "Knowing and Not Knowing," 255; Cohen, *States of Denial*, xii. See also Frank Graziano, *Divine Violence: Spectacle, Psychosexuality, and Radical Christianity in the Argentine "Dirty War"* (Boulder, CO: Westview, 1992), 79, 255–56.

22. Horwitz, *In the Shadow of Death*, 35. See also 36–37, 92–93, 96.

23. Ibid., 94 [emphasis added]. See also Martin Amis, *Koba the Dread: Laughter and the Twenty Million* (New York: Hyperion, 2002), 39.

24. Zali Gurevitch, "Dialectical Dialogue: The Struggle for Speech, Repressive Silence, and the Shift to Multiplicity," *British Journal of Sociology* 52 (2001), 93; Adam Jaworski, *The Power of Silence: Social and Pragmatic Perspectives* (Newbury Park, CA: Sage, 1993), 135; George Orwell, *Nineteen Eighty-Four* (New York: New American Library, 1961 [1949]), 122. See also Graziano, *Divine Violence*, 255–56; Luchterhand, "Knowing and Not Knowing," 262; Horwitz, *In the Shadow of Death*, 114; Peter Haidu, "The Dialectics of Unspeakability: Language, Silence, and the Narratives of Desubjectification," in Saul Friedlander (ed.), *Probing the Limits of Representation: Nazism and the "Final Solution"* (Cambridge, MA: Harvard University Press, 1992), 277–99; Dariusz Tolczyk, *See No Evil: Literary Cover-Ups and Discoveries of the Soviet Camp*

Experience (New Haven, CT: Yale University Press, 1999), 180–83; Cohen, *States of Denial*, 154.

25. Georg Simmel, "The Secret and the Secret Society," in Kurt H. Wolff (ed.), *The Sociology of Georg Simmel* (New York: Free Press, 1950 [1908]), 307–76; Sissela Bok, *Secrets: On the Ethics of Concealment and Revelation* (New York: Vintage Books, 1989 [1983]).

26. Jeffrey Gettleman, "Thurmond Family Struggles with Difficult Truth," *New York Times*, December 20, 2003, A13.

27. Laurie Goodstein, "Lawyer for Church Says He Hid His Own Sexual Abuse by Priest," *New York Times*, November 25, 2003, A1.

28. "Ending Legal Secrecy," *New York Times*, September 5, 2002, A22.

29. Ibid. See also Thomas Farragher, "Church Cloaked in Culture of Silence," *Boston Globe*, February 24, 2002, www.pulitzer.org/year/2003/public-service/works/globe9.html

30. Walter V. Robinson, "Scores of Priests Involved in Sex Abuse Cases: Settlements Kept Scope of Issue Out of Public Eye," *Boston Globe*, January 31, 2002, www.pulitzer.org/year/2003/public-service/works/globe5.html

31. See also Adam Liptak, "South Carolina Judges Voted to Ban Secret Court Settlements," *New York Times*, September 2, 2002, A1; "Ending Legal Secrecy."

32. Alice M. Earle, *Curious Punishments of Bygone Days* (Chicago: Herbert F. Stone & Co., 1896), 96–101.

33. Pat Conroy, *The Prince of Tides* (New York: Bantam, 2002 [1986]), 500.

34. Eviatar Zerubavel, *Terra Cognita: The Mental Discovery of America* (New Brunswick, NJ: Rutgers University Press, 1992), 89–90.

35. The Office of the Independent Counsel, "Referral to the United States House of Representatives Pursuant to Title 28, United States Code, § 595(C)" [also known as "The Starr Report"], #731–59, *New York Times*, September 12, 1998, B7. See also David E. Sanger, "Lewinsky Was Familiar Face to Agents near Clinton's Door," *New York Times*, September 13, 1998, National Section, 35.
36. Hans Christian Andersen, "The Emperor's New Clothes," in *The Complete Fairy Tales and Stories* (Garden City, NY: Doubleday, 1974 [1836]), 77.
37. See also Tamar Cohen, "Incest: On Keeping the Secret," in Hanna Herzog and Kineret Lahad (eds.), *Knowing and Remaining Silent: Mechanisms of Silencing and Denial in Israeli Society* (Jerusalem: Van Leer Institute, forthcoming).

Chapter Four

1. Eviatar Zerubavel, "The Elephant in the Room: Notes on the Social Organization of Denial," in Karen A. Cerulo (ed.), *Culture in Mind: Toward a Sociology of Culture and Cognition* (New York: Routledge, 2002), 25.
2. Robin E. Sheriff, "Exposing Silence as Cultural Censorship: A Brazilian Case," *American Anthropologist* 102 (2000), 114. See also I. F. Stone, "It Pays To Be Ignorant," *New York Review of Books*, August 9, 1973, 8; Stanley Cohen, *States of Denial: Knowing about Atrocities and Suffering* (Cambridge: Polity, 2001), 64–65, 125; Donald Cozzens, *Sacred Silence: Denial and the Crisis in the Church* (Collegeville, MN: The Liturgical Press, 2002), 41.
3. Frederick B. Bird, *The Muted Conscience: Moral Silence and the Practice of Ethics in Business* (Westport, CT: Quorum Books, 1996), 191, 194.

4. David E. Sanger, "Lewinsky Was Familiar Face to Agents near Clinton's Door," *New York Times*, September 13, 1998, National Section, 35.

5. Stephen J. Dubner, "Steven the Good," *New York Times*, February 14, 1999, section 6, 38.

6. Jan E. Lewis, "The White Jeffersons," in Jan E. Lewis and Peter S. Onuf (eds.), *Sally Hemings and Thomas Jefferson: History, Memory, and Civic Culture* (Charlottesville: University Press of Virginia, 1999), 154; Erving Goffman, *The Presentation of Self in Everyday Life* (Garden City, NY: Doubleday Anchor, 1959), 234–37; Erving Goffman, "On Face Work: An Analysis of Ritual Elements in Social Interaction," in *Interaction Ritual: Essays on Face-to-Face Behavior* (Garden City, NY: Doubleday Anchor, 1967 [1955]), 29; Raymond Geuss, *Public Goods, Private Goods* (Princeton, NJ: Princeton University Press, 2001), 13–14.

7. Gordon J. Horwitz, *In the Shadow of Death: Living Outside the Gates of Mauthausen* (New York: Free Press, 1990), 175. See also Derrick Jensen, *A Language Older Than Words* (New York: Context Books, 2000), 347.

8. Dan Bar-On, *Legacy of Silence: Encounters with Children of the Third Reich* (Cambridge, MA: Harvard University Press, 1989), 328; Ruth Wajnryb, *The Silence: How Tragedy Shapes Talk* (Crows Nest, Australia: Allen & Unwin, 2001), 32, 265; Martin Goldsmith, *The Inextinguishable Symphony: A True Story of Music and Love in Nazi Germany* (New York: John Wiley & Sons, 2000), 2. See also Nadine Fresco, "Remembering the Unknown," *International Review of Psycho-Analysis* 11 (1984), 418.

9. Mark Jordan, *The Silence of Sodom: Homosexuality in Modern Catholicism* (Chicago: University of Chicago Press, 2000), 90, 107.

10. Barney G. Glaser and Anselm L. Strauss, *Awareness of Dying* (Chicago: University of Chicago Press, 1965), 125, 67; Daniel Goleman, *Vital Lies, Simple Truths: The Psychology of Self-Deception* (New York: Touchstone Books, 1986), 157; Cohen, *States of Denial*, 66; Diane Vaughan, *Uncoupling: Turning Points in Intimate Relationships* (New York: Oxford University Press, 1986), 64, 76–78. See also Dan Bar-On, *The Indescribable and the Undiscussable: Reconstructing Human Discourse after Trauma* (Budapest: Central European University Press, 1999), 162.

11. Philip Vellacott, *Sophocles and Oedipus: A Study of Oedipus Tyrannus with a New Translation* (Ann Arbor: University of Michigan Press, 1971), 24–25, 115–17, 156–57, 163, 171, 173, 185–86, 220, 224. See also John Steiner, "Turning a Blind Eye: The Cover Up for Oedipus," *International Review of Psycho-Analysis* 12 (1985), 165–66, 168; John Steiner, *Psychic Retreats: Pathological Organisations in Psychotic, Neurotic, and Borderline Patients* (London: Routledge, 1993), 120–21; Noam Zerubavel, "Allegorical Recognition of Truth and Identity in *Oedipus Rex*" (Columbia University, 2003).

12. Kathleen Gerson, personal communication.

13 Randy Shilts, *And the Band Played On: Politics, People, and the AIDS Epidemic* (New York: St. Martin's Press, 1987); Kathryn Harrison, *The Kiss* (New York: Avon Books, 1997), 117.

14. Elizabeth W. Morrison and Frances J. Milliken, "Organizational Silence: A Barrier to Change and Development in a Pluralistic World," *Academy of Management Review* 25 (2000), 721. See also 722; Chris Argyris, "Skilled Incompetence," *Harvard Business Review*, September–October 1986, 76.

15. Jordan, *The Silence of Sodom*, 87. See also Sissela Bok, *Secrets: On the Ethics of Concealment and Revelation* (New York: Vintage Books, 1989 [1983]), xiii.

16. Fred C. Alford, *Whistleblowers: Broken Lives and Organizational Power* (Ithaca, NY: Cornell University Press, 2001), 20–21.

17. Ronald D. Laing, "The Politics of the Family," in *The Politics of the Family and Other Essays* (New York: Pantheon Books, 1971 [1969]), 99–100, 106, 115; Goleman, *Vital Lies, Simple Truths*, 234; George Orwell, *Nineteen Eighty-Four* (New York: New American Library, 1961 [1949]), 33, 150.

18. Hans Christian Andersen, "The Emperor's New Clothes," in *The Complete Fairy Tales and Stories* (Garden City, NY: Doubleday, 1974 [1836]), 81.

19. Georg Simmel, "The Secret and the Secret Society," in Kurt H. Wolff (ed.), *The Sociology of Georg Simmel* (New York: Free Press, 1950 [1908]), 332; Eviatar Zerubavel, "Personal Information and Social Life," *Symbolic Interaction* 5, no. 1 (1982), 101–02.

20. Cohen, *States of Denial*, 15–18, 68–75, 140–67. See also Georg Simmel, "Quantitative Aspects of the Group," in Kurt H. Wolff, *The Sociology of Georg Simmel* (New York: Free Press, 1950 [1908]), 135–36, 145–69.

21. See also Bibb Latané and John M. Darley, *The Unresponsive Bystander: Why Doesn't He Help?* (New York: Appleton-Century-Crofts, 1970); Pavel Machotka et al., "Incest as a Family Affair," *Family Process* 6 (1967), 99–100; Dan Bar-On, *The Indescribable and the Undiscussable: Reconstructing Human Discourse after Trauma* (Budapest: Central European University Press, 1999), 199.

22. See Solomon E. Asch, "Studies of Independence and Conformity: A Minority of One against a Unanimous Majority," *Psychological Monographs* 70 (1956), #9 (whole no. 416); Muzafer Sherif and Carolyn W. Sherif, *Social Psychology* (New York: Harper and Row, 1969), 70–72, 119–21,

202–10; Robert B. Cialdini, *Influence: Science and Practice* (New York: HarperCollins, 1993), 94–133.

23. Henrik Ibsen, "An Enemy of the People," in *Six Plays by Henrik Ibsen* (New York: The Modern Library, 1957 [1882]), 225. See also 226–27.

24. Ethel M. Albert, "Culture Patterning of Speech Behavior in Burundi," in John J. Gumperz and Dell Hymes (eds.), *Directions in Sociolinguistics: The Ethnography of Communication* (New York: Holt, Rinehart and Winston, 1972), 91; Morrison and Milliken, "Organizational Silence," 706. See also Nina Eliasoph, *Avoiding Politics: How Americans Produce Apathy in Everyday Life* (Cambridge: Cambridge University Press, 1998).

25. On the fundamental distinction between social statics and social dynamics, see Auguste Comte, *Cours de Philosophie Positive*, in Gertrud Lenzer (ed.), *Auguste Comte and Positivism: The Essential Writings* (New York: Harper Torchbooks, 1975 [1830–42]), 263–97.

26. Andersen, "The Emperor's New Clothes," 79. See also Helen S. Perry, "Selective Inattention as an Explanatory Concept for U.S. Public Attitudes toward the Atomic Bomb," *Psychiatry* 17 (1954), 226.

27. Paul Simon, "The Sound of Silence," 1964.

28. Bird, *The Muted Conscience*, 51. See also Stanley Milgram, *Obedience to Authority: An Experimental View* (New York: Harper and Row, 1974), 149; Zygmunt Bauman, *Modernity and the Holocaust* (Ithaca, NY: Cornell University Press, 2000 [1989]), 158.

29. Rudolf Flesch, *The New Book of Unusual Quotations* (New York: Harper and Row, 1966), 349–50 [emphasis added]; Kathleen D. Ryan and Daniel K. Oestreich, *Driving Fear Out of the Office: How To Overcome the Invisible Barriers to Quality,*

Productivity, and Innovation (San Francisco: Jossey-Bass, 1991), 30; Jane Smiley, *A Thousand Acres* (New York: Fawcett Columbine, 1991).

30. Goldsmith, *The Inextinguishable Symphony*, 2.

Chapter Five

1. *New Yorker*, August 2, 1976, 19.
2. See also Judith L. Herman, *Trauma and Recovery* (New York: BasicBooks, 1992), 1.
3. On the clothes dryer, see also Ronald G. Klietsch, "Clothes-line Patterns and Covert Behavior," *Journal of Marriage and the Family* 27 (1965), 78–80.
4. Aleksandr Solzhenitsyn, *One Day in the Life of Ivan Denisovich* (New York: Praeger, 1963 [1962]); Benny Morris, *The Birth of the Palestinian Refugee Problem, 1947–1949* (New York: Cambridge University Press, 1987). See also Yitzhak Laor, "We Write You, Homeland," in *Narratives with No Natives: Essays on Israeli Literature* (Tel Aviv: Hotzaat Hakibbutz Hameuchad, 1995), 133.
5. Donald Cozzens, *Sacred Silence: Denial and the Crisis in the Church* (Collegeville, MN: The Liturgical Press, 2002), 6, 8; Shoshana Felman and Dori Laub (eds.), *Testimony: Crises of Witnessing in Literature, Psychoanalysis, and History* (New York: Routledge, 1992); Helena Roche, *The Addiction Process: From Enabling to Intervention* (Deerfield Beach, FL: Health Communications, 1990). See also Robert K. White, "Family Intervention: Background, Principles, and Other Strategies," in Robert K. White and Deborah G. Wright (eds.), *Addiction Intervention: Strategies to Motivate Treatment-Seeking Behavior* (New York: Haworth Press, 1998), 12;

Stanley Cohen, *States of Denial: Knowing about Atrocities and Suffering* (Cambridge: Polity, 2001), 222–77.

6. Larry Gross, *Contested Closets: The Politics and Ethics of Outing* (Minneapolis: University of Minnesota Press, 1993); Warren Johansson and William A. Percy, *Outing: Shattering the Conspiracy of Silence* (Binghamton, NY: Haworth Press, 1994); Lynette Clemetson, "Proposed Marriage Ban Splits Washington's Gays," *New York Times*, July 25, 2004, A17.

7. Rolf Hochhuth, *The Deputy* (New York: Grove Press, 1964 [1963]).

8. On "backstage" regions of social life, see Erving Goffman, *The Presentation of Self in Everyday Life* (Garden City, NY: Doubleday Anchor, 1959), 112–40.

9. See also Herbert Fingarette, *Self-Deception* (London: Routledge & Kegan Paul, 1969), 39–51; Alina Kwiatkowska, "Silence across Modalities," in Adam Jaworski (ed.), *Silence: Interdisciplinary Perspectives* (Berlin and New York: Mouton de Gruyter, 1997), 330; Dan Bar-On, *The Indescribable and the Undiscussable: Reconstructing Human Discourse after Trauma* (Budapest: Central European University Press, 1999), 165; Larraine Segil, *Dynamic Leader, Adaptive Organization: Ten Essential Traits for Managers* (New York: John Wiley & Sons, 2002), 125.

10. Cohen, *States of Denial*, 251; Barbie Zelizer, *Remembering to Forget: Holocaust Memory through the Camera's Eye* (Chicago: University of Chicago Press, 1998), 136–37. See also Segil, *Dynamic Leader, Adaptive Organization*, 3–4, 125.

11. Genesis 3: 5–7.

12. Nurit Wurgaft, "She Turns On the Mike and Lifts Up the Rug," *Haaretz*, May 31, 2004, www.haaretz.com/hasen/pages/ShArt.jhtml?itemNo=431602&contrassID=2&subContrassID=20&sbSubContrassID=0&listSrc=Y See also Jill Wagner, "Arab Talk Radio Host Seeks To Break

Taboos," *MSNBC News* (online edition), July 22, 2004, http://thejuice.msnbc.com/id/5466283

13. "Moore Fires Oscar Anti-War Salvo," March 24, 2003, http://news.bbc.co.uk/1/hi/entertainment/film/2879857.stm

14. See, for example, Kathryn Harrison, *The Kiss* (New York: Avon Books, 1997); Boston Women's Health Book Collective, *Our Bodies, Ourselves: A Book by and for Women* (New York: Simon and Schuster, 1973); Irshad Manji, *The Trouble with Islam: A Muslim's Call for Reform in Her Faith* (Toronto: Random House of Canada, 2003); Hanna Naveh, "The Marital Bed," in Hanna Herzog and Kineret Lahad (eds.), *Knowing and Remaining Silent: Mechanisms of Silencing and Denial in Israeli Society* (Jerusalem: Van Leer Institute, forthcoming); Harold Garfinkel, "Studies of the Routine Grounds of Everyday Activities," in *Studies in Ethnomethodology* (Englewood Cliffs, NJ: Prentice-Hall, 1967 [1964]), 35–75; Eviatar Zerubavel, *The Seven-Day Circle: The History and Meaning of the Week* (Chicago: University of Chicago Press, 1989 [1985]); Wayne Brekhus, "A Sociology of the Unmarked: Redirecting Our Focus," *Sociological Theory* 16 (1998), 34–51; Eric Klinenberg, *Heat Wave: A Social Autopsy of Disaster in Chicago* (Chicago: University of Chicago Press, 2002).

15. Nadine Fresco, "Remembering the Unknown," *International Review of Psycho-Analysis* 11 (1984), 419; Betty Friedan, *The Feminine Mystique* (New York: W. W. Norton, 1963), 15; *Nightline*, April 30, 2004; "Clinton's 'Hunker-Down' Strategy Holds: President Sidesteps Most Things Lewinsky at Press Conference with U.K.'s Blair," www.cnn.com/ALLPOLITICS/1998/02/06/clinton.blair.presser; "President Bill Clinton, Prime Minister Tony Blair Joint News Conference—Feb. 6, 1998," www.cnn.com/ALLPOLITICS/1998/02/06/transcripts/clinton See also Tamar Katriel,

Talking Straight: Dugri Speech in Israeli Sabra Culture (Cambridge: Cambridge University Press, 1986); Brekhus, "A Sociology of the Unmarked," 35–36.

16. www.arlingtonwestfilm.com See also www.breaking thesilence.org.il/index_en.asp

17. *The Daily Show with Jon Stewart*, July 28, 2003.

18. Fritz K. M. Hillenbrandt, *Underground Humour in Nazi Germany 1933–1945* (London: Routledge, 1995), 11. See also the cartoon on 37.

19. See Marguerite G. Bouvard, *Revolutionizing Motherhood: The Mothers of the Plaza de Mayo* (Wilmington, DE: Scholarly Resources Inc., 1994).

20. See also Kanan Makiya, *Cruelty and Silence: War, Tyranny, Uprising, and the Arab World* (New York: W. W. Norton, 1993), 25.

21. Vernon E. Johnson, *Intervention: How To Help Someone Who Doesn't Want Help* (Minneapolis, MN: Johnson Institute Books, 1986), 66. See also Vernon E. Johnson, *I'll Quit Tomorrow* (New York: Harper and Row, 1973), 50; Roche, *The Addiction Process*, 189, 193.

22. See Malcolm Gladwell, *The Tipping Point: How Little Things Can Make a Big Difference* (New York: Little, Brown, and Co., 2000).

23. *Time*, December 30, 2002–January 6, 2003, 59.

24. Jerry L. Avorn et al., *Up against the Ivy Wall: A History of the Columbia Crisis* (New York: Atheneum, 1969), 28 [emphasis added].

25. Hans Christian Andersen, "The Emperor's New Clothes," in *The Complete Fairy Tales and Stories* (Garden City, NY: Doubleday, 1974 [1836]), 81.

26. Cynthia Crossen, "Know Thy Father," *Wall Street Journal*, March 4, 1997, A16.

27. Alan F. Westin, "Introduction," in Alan F. Westin (ed.), *Whistle Blowing: Loyalty and Dissent in the Corporation* (New York: McGraw-Hill, 1981), 1–15; Myron P. Glazer and Penina M. Glazer, *The Whistleblowers: Exposing Corruption in Government and Industry* (New York: Basic Books, 1989), 133–66; James M. Jasper, *The Art of Moral Protest: Culture, Biography, and Creativity in Social Movements* (Chicago: University of Chicago Press, 1997), 139; Joyce Rothschild and Terence D. Miethe, "Whistle-Blower Disclosures and Management Retaliation: The Battle to Control Information about Organization Corruption," *Work and Occupations* 26 (1999), 120; C. Fred Alford, *Whistleblowers: Broken Lives and Organizational Power* (Ithaca, NY: Cornell University Press, 2001), 18.

Chapter Six

1. Don Juan Manuel, "What Happened to the King and the Tricksters Who Made Cloth," in John E. Keller and L. Clark Keating (trans.), *The Book of Count Lucanor and Patronio* (Lexington: University Press of Kentucky, 1977 [1335]), 132.
2. See also Serge Moscovici, "Social Influence and Conformity," in Gardner Lindzey and Elliot Aronson (eds.), *Handbook of Social Psychology* (New York: Random House, 1985), vol. 2, 385–96; Thomas E. DeGloma, "'Safe Space' and Contested Memories: Survivor Movements and the Foundation of Alternative Mnemonic Traditions," presented at the "Spaces of Memory, Spaces of Violence" conference, New School University, New York, April 2004.
3. Eleonora Lev, "Lolita: Her Real Story," *Ha'aretz Literary Supplement*, October 7, 1998, 5 [emphasis added].

4. Michael Stohl, "Outside of a Small Circle of Friends: States, Genocide, Mass Killing and the Role of Bystanders," *Journal of Peace Research* 24 (1987), 159; John Lennon and Paul McCartney, "Strawberry Fields Forever," 1966. See also Kari M. Norgaard, "People Want To Protect Themselves A Little Bit: Emotions, Denial and Social Movement Non-Participation—The Case of Global Climate Change," presented at the annual meeting of the American Sociological Association, Atlanta, August 2003.

5. See also Erving Goffman, "On Face Work: An Analysis of Ritual Elements in Social Interaction," in *Interaction Ritual: Essays on Face-to-Face Behavior* (Garden City, NY: Doubleday Anchor, 1967 [1955]), 5–45; Penelope Brown and Stephen C. Levinson, *Politeness: Some Universals in Language Use* (Cambridge: Cambridge University Press, 1987 [1978]); Linn Van Dyne et al., "Conceptualizing Employee Silence and Employee Voice as Multidimensional Constructs," *Journal of Management Studies* 40 (2003), 1368.

6. See also Eviatar Zerubavel, "Personal Information and Social Life," *Symbolic Interaction* 5, no. 1 (1982), 107; Chalda Maloff and Susan M. Wood, *Business and Social Etiquette with Disabled People: A Guide to Getting Along with Persons Who Have Impairments of Mobility, Vision, Hearing, or Speech* (Springfield, IL: Charles C. Thomas, 1988), 42, 88; Shoshana Felman and Dori Laub (eds.), *Testimony: Crises of Witnessing in Literature, Psychoanalysis, and History* (New York: Routledge, 1992), 83.

7. Chuck 45, "An Elephant in their Midst," October 9, 2000, www.thegully.com/essays/gaymundo/001009 elephant.html; "Cheney's Daughter a Flash Point," *CBS News* (online edition), October 15, 2004, www. cbsnews.com/stories/2004/10/15/politics/main649514.shtml

8. See also *Babylonian Talmud, Bava Mesia*, chap. 4, folio 59b [in Jacob Neusner (trans.) *The Talmud of Babylonia* (Atlanta:

Scholars Press, 1990), vol. 21, part B, 157]; Ralph K. White et al., "Studies in Adjustment to Visible Injuries: Evaluation of Curiosity by the Injured," *Journal of Abnormal and Social Psychology* 43 (1948), 19; Thomas J. Bruneau, "Communicative Silences: Forms and Functions," *Journal of Communication* 23 (1973), 32; Erving Goffman, *Frame Analysis: An Essay on the Organization of Experience* (New York: Harper Colophon, 1974), 204; Judith Martin, *Miss Manners' Guide for the Turn-of-the-Millennium* (New York: Fireside, 1990), 306; Adam Jaworski, *The Power of Silence: Social and Pragmatic Perspectives* (Newbury Park, CA: Sage, 1993), 59–61.

9. See also Mary P. Baumgartner, *The Moral Order of a Suburb* (New York: Oxford University Press, 1988), 60–66, 73–82; Deborah Tannen, "Silence as Conflict Management in Fiction and Drama: Pinter's *Betrayal* and a Short Story, 'Great Wits,'" in Allen D. Grimshaw (ed.), *Conflict Talk: Sociolinguistic Investigations of Arguments in Conversations* (Cambridge: Cambridge University Press, 1990), 260–79.

10. See also Terence D. Miethe, *Whistleblowing at Work: Tough Choices in Exposing Fraud, Waste, and Abuse on the Job* (Boulder, CO: Westview, 1999), 11–12, 21–23.

11. Sanford Pinsker, "Art as Excess: The 'Voices' of Charlie Parker and Philip Roth," *Partisan Review* 69 (2002), 60; Jeffrey M. Masson, *The Assault on Truth: Freud's Suppression of the Seduction Theory* (New York: Farrar, Straus and Giroux, 1984), xv–xxiii; Christopher J. Farley, "What Bill Cosby Should Be Talking About," *Time* (online edition), June 3, 2004, www.time.com/time/nation/article/0,8599,645801,00.html [emphasis added]; www.filmstew.com/Content/details Printer.asp?ContentID=8896 [emphasis added].

12. See also Peter Faulkner, "Exposing Risks of Nuclear Disaster," in Alan F. Westin (ed.), *Whistle Blowing: Loyalty and Dissent in the Corporation* (New York: McGraw-Hill, 1981), 42; Sissela Bok, *Secrets: On the Ethics of Concealment and*

Revelation (New York: Vintage Books, 1989 [1983]), 213–14; W. Charles Redding, "Rocking Boats, Blowing Whistles, and Teaching Speech Communication," *Communication Education* 34 (1985), 245–58; Jo Sprague and Gary L. Ruud, "Boat Rocking in the High-Technology Culture," *American Behavioral Scientist* 32 (1988), 169–93; Kathleen D. Ryan and Daniel K. Oestreich, *Driving Fear Out of the Office: How To Overcome the Invisible Barriers to Quality, Productivity, and Innovation* (San Francisco: Jossey-Bass, 1991), 43–44; Marcia P. Miceli and Janet P. Near, *Blowing the Whistle: The Organizational and Legal Implications for Companies and Employees* (New York: Lexington, 1992), 81–83.

13. Michel Foucault, *The History of Sexuality* (New York: Pantheon, 1978 [1976]), vol. 1, 6.

14. Czesław Miłosz, Nobel Prize acceptance speech, 1980. See http://nobelprize.org/literature/laureates/1980/milosz-lecture-en.html

15. Sandra Butler, *Conspiracy of Silence: The Trauma of Incest* (San Francisco: Volcano Press, 1985), 142. See also Pavel Machotka et al., "Incest as a Family Affair," *Family Process* 6 (1967), 100.

16. Kate F. Hays, "The Conspiracy of Silence Revisited: Group Therapy with Adult Survivors of Incest," *Journal of Group Psychotherapy, Psychodrama, and Sociometry* 39 (1987), 143. See also Bok, *Secrets*, 309.

Chapter Seven

1. Nancy V. Raine, *After Silence: Rape and My Journey Back* (New York: Crown, 1998), 121 [emphasis added].

2. Kathryn Harrison, *The Kiss* (New York: Avon Books, 1997), 86.

3. Ibid., 74 [emphasis added].
4. Eviatar Zerubavel, *Social Mindscapes: An Invitation to Cognitive Sociology* (Cambridge, MA: Harvard University Press, 1997), 83–84. See also Thomas E. DeGloma, "Memory and the Cognitive Masking of Child Sex Abuse: Framing and Cognitive Asymmetries of Power in the Family," presented at the annual meeting of the American Sociological Association, Atlanta, August 2003.
5. Marion H. Typpo and Jill M. Hastings, *An Elephant in the Living Room: A Leader's Guide for Helping Children of Alcoholics* (Center City, MN: Hazelden, 1984), ii. See also 16.
6. Anonymous nursery rhyme presumably based on a very similar poem by Ogden Nash.
7. Eric D. Lister, "Forced Silence: A Neglected Dimension of Trauma," *American Journal of Psychiatry* 139 (1982), 872–76; Judith L. Herman, "Foreword," in Sandra Butler, *Conspiracy of Silence: The Trauma of Incest* (San Francisco: Volcano Press, 1985), ix; Ruth Wajnryb, *The Silence: How Tragedy Shapes Talk* (Crows Nest, Australia: Allen & Unwin, 2001), 104, 191.
8. Gordon W. Allport, "Foreword," in Norman L. Farberow (ed.), *Taboo Topics* (New York: Atheling Books, 1966 [1963]), vi; Kathleen D. Ryan and Daniel K. Oestreich, *Driving Fear Out of the Office: How To Overcome the Invisible Barriers to Quality, Productivity, and Innovation* (San Francisco: Jossey-Bass, 1991), 31, 35, 185.
9. Hans Christian Andersen, "The Emperor's New Clothes," in *The Complete Fairy Tales and Stories* (Garden City, NY: Doubleday, 1974 [1836]), 79 [emphasis added].
10. George Orwell, *Nineteen Eighty-Four* (New York: New American Library, 1961 [1949]), 32.
11. Robert J. Lifton, *The Nazi Doctors: Medical Killing and the Psychology of Genocide* (New York: Basic Books, 1986), 203,

445. See also 442–47; Robert J. Lifton, "Imagining the Real," in Robert J. Lifton and Richard Falk (eds.), *Indefensible Weapons: The Political and Psychological Case against Nuclearism* (New York: Basic Books, 1982), 100–110; Arlie Hochschild, *The Managed Heart: Commercialization of Human Feeling* (Berkeley: University of California Press, 1983); Judith L. Herman, *Trauma and Recovery* (New York: Basic Books, 1992), 1; Robert J. Lifton and Greg Mitchell, *Hiroshima in America: Fifty Years of Denial* (New York: G. P. Putnam's Sons, 1995), 337–40; Derrick Jensen, *A Language Older Than Words* (New York: Context Books, 2000), 3.

12. Harrison, *The Kiss*, 75.

13. Zerubavel, *Social Mindscapes*, 6–8.

14. Thomas Mann, *The Magic Mountain* (New York: Vintage Books, 1969 [1924]), 518. See also Wajnryb, *The Silence*, 77–78.

15. Terry Kettering, "The Elephant in the Room."

16. Mark Jordan, *The Silence of Sodom: Homosexuality in Modern Catholicism* (Chicago: University of Chicago Press, 2000), 89; Betty Friedan, *The Feminine Mystique* (New York: W. W. Norton, 1963), 19.

17. See, for example, Sandra Butler, *Conspiracy of Silence: The Trauma of Incest* (San Francisco: Volcano Press, 1985), 8, 188–90; Raine, *After Silence*, 126; Susan J. Brison, *Aftermath: Violence and the Remaking of a Self* (Princeton, NJ: Princeton University Press, 2002), 51, 56–59, 98.

18. Pat Conroy, *The Prince of Tides* (New York: Bantam, 2002 [1986]), 500–501.

19. Kate F. Hays, "The Conspiracy of Silence Revisited: Group Therapy with Adult Survivors of Incest," *Journal of Group Psychotherapy, Psychodrama, and Sociometry* 39 (1987), 143–56; Brison, *Aftermath*, xi; Thomas E. DeGloma, "'Safe Space' and Contested Memories: Survivor Movements and the

Foundation of Alternative Mnemonic Traditions," presented at the "Spaces of Memory, Spaces of Violence" conference, New School University, New York, April 2004.

20. Donald A. Bloch, "Foreword," in David S. Greenwald and Steven J. Zeitlin, *No Reason To Talk About It: Families Confront the Nuclear Taboo* (New York: W. W. Norton, 1987), viii [emphasis added].

21. Wajnryb, *The Silence*, 249. See also 46.

22. Terry Kettering, "The Elephant in the Room."

23. Dan Bar-On, *The Indescribable and the Undiscussable: Reconstructing Human Discourse after Trauma* (Budapest: Central European University Press, 1999), 158; Frederick B. Bird, *The Muted Conscience: Moral Silence and the Practice of Ethics in Business* (Westport, CT: Quorum Books, 1996), 141.

24. Bloch, "Foreword" to Greenwald and Zeitlin's *No Reason To Talk About It*, viii; Sylvia Fraser, *My Father's House: A Memoir of Incest and of Healing* (New York: Perennial Library, 1989 [1987]), 239–40. See also Bar-On, *The Indescribable and the Undiscussable*, 200–202, 210–15.

25. See also Chris Argyris, "Skilled Incompetence," *Harvard Business Review*, September–October 1986, 76; Jo Sprague and Gary L. Ruud, "Boat Rocking in the High-Technology Culture," *American Behavioral Scientist* 32 (1988), 172; Ryan and Oestreich, *Driving Fear Out of the Office*, 36; Elizabeth W. Morrison and Frances J. Milliken, "Organizational Silence: A Barrier to Change and Development in a Pluralistic World," *Academy of Management Review* 25 (2000), 719; Larraine Segil, *Dynamic Leader, Adaptive Organization: Ten Essential Traits for Managers* (New York: John Wiley & Sons, 2002).

26. Donald Cozzens, *Sacred Silence: Denial and the Crisis in the Church* (Collegeville, MN: The Liturgical Press, 2002), 62; Sissela Bok, *Secrets: On the Ethics of Concealment and Revelation* (New York: Vintage Books, 1989 [1983]), xv; Herman,

Trauma and Recovery, 7–8; Kanan Makiya, *Cruelty and Silence: War, Tyranny, Uprising, and the Arab World* (New York: W. W. Norton, 1993), 287. See also Bird, *The Muted Conscience*, 49–53.

27. See also Judith L. Herman, *Father-Daughter Incest* (Cambridge, MA: Harvard University Press, 1981), 135; Jennifer J. Freyd, *Betrayal Trauma: The Logic of Forgetting Childhood Abuse* (Cambridge, MA: Harvard University Press, 1996), 162.

28. *Playgirl*, August 1978, 9.

29. A 1965 poem by Günter Kunert, in Wolfgang Mieder, *Tradition and Innovation in Folk Literature* (Hanover, NH: University Press of New England, 1987), 173. See also 174 as well as the political cartoons on 170–73.

30. James M. Jasper, *The Art of Moral Protest: Culture, Biography, and Creativity in Social Movements* (Chicago: University of Chicago Press, 1997), 139; Leonard R. Frank, (ed.). *Random House Webster's Quotationary* (New York: Random House, 1998), 788; Jacobo Timerman, *Prisoner Without a Name, Cell Without a Number* (New York: Alfred A. Knopf, 1981), 141. See also Makiya, *Cruelty and Silence*; Stanley Cohen, *States of Denial: Knowing about Atrocities and Suffering* (Cambridge: Polity, 2001).

31. See also David S. Greenwald and Steven J. Zeitlin, *No Reason To Talk about It: Families Confront the Nuclear Taboo* (New York: W. W. Norton, 1987), 15; Mica Pollock, *Colormute: Race Talk Dilemmas in an American School* (Princeton, NJ: Princeton University Press, 2004), 170.

32. Jon Entine, *Taboo: Why Black Athletes Dominate Sports and Why We're Afraid To Talk about It* (New York: PublicAffairs, 2000), 10.

33. Betsy Petersen, *Dancing with Daddy: A Childhood Lost and a Life Regained* (New York: Bantam, 1991), 57–58. On elephants' infamously foul smell, see Audrey Hudson, "Biologists' Roles

in Lynx-Hair Fraud under Review," *Washington Times*, April 23, 2002; Segil, *Dynamic Leader, Adaptive Organization*, 3. See also the cartoon in Mike Peters, *The Nixon Chronicles* (Dayton, OH: Lorenz Press, 1976), 81.

34. Shamai Davidson, "The Clinical Effects of Massive Psychic Trauma in Families of Holocaust Survivors," *Journal of Marital and Family Therapy* 6 (1980), 14, 19; Sylvia Axelrod et al., "Hospitalized Offspring of Holocaust Survivors," *Bulletin of the Menninger Clinic* 44 (1980), 12; Bar-On, *The Indescribable and the Undiscussable*, 200–202, 210–15; Hadas Wiseman et al., "Parental Communication of Holocaust Experiences and Interpersonal Patterns in Offspring of Holocaust Survivors," *International Journal of Behavioral Development* 26 (2002), 371–81.

35. Pavel Machotka et al., "Incest as a Family Affair," *Family Process* 6 (1967), 113–15. See also Bloch, "Foreword" to Greenwald and Zeitlin's *No Reason To Talk About It*, vii; Jensen, *A Language Older Than Words*, 4.

36. *CBS News*, January 6, 2005, http://election.cbsnews.com/ stories/2005/01/06/world/main665228.shtml

Bibliography

Adair, Bill, and Katherine Gazella. "It Lasted 72 Minutes Without a Mention." *St. Petersburg Times*, January 28, 1998, A8.

Adams, Robert M. "Soft Soap and the Nitty-Gritty." In *Fair of Speech: The Uses of Euphemism*, ed. D. J. Enright, 44–55. Oxford: Oxford University Press, 1985.

Albert, Ethel M. "Culture Patterning of Speech Behavior in Burundi." In *Directions in Sociolinguistics: The Ethnography of Communication*, ed. John J. Gumperz and Dell Hymes, 72–105. New York: Holt, Rinehart and Winston, 1972.

Alford, C. Fred. *Whistleblowers: Broken Lives and Organizational Power*. Ithaca, NY: Cornell University Press, 2001.

Allan, Keith, and Kate Burridge. *Euphemism and Dysphemism: Language Used as Shield and Weapon*. New York: Oxford University Press, 1991.

Allport, Gordon W. "Foreword." In *Taboo Topics*, ed. Norman L. Farberow, v–x. New York: Atheling Books, 1966 [1963].

Amis, Martin. *Koba the Dread: Laughter and the Twenty Million*. New York: Hyperion, 2002.

Andersen, Hans Christian. "The Emperor's New Clothes." In *The Complete Fairy Tales and Stories*, 77–81. Garden City, NY: Doubleday, 1974 [1836].

Andreyev, Leonid N. "Silence." In *The Little Angel and Other Stories*, 121–47. Freeport, NY: Books for Libraries Press, 1971 [1910].

Argyris, Chris. "Skilled Incompetence." *Harvard Business Review*, September–October 1986, 74–79.

Asch, Solomon E. "Studies of Independence and Conformity: A Minority of One against a Unanimous Majority." *Psychological Monographs* 70 (1956), #9 (whole no. 416).

Avorn, Jerry L., et al. *Up against the Ivy Wall: A History of the Columbia Crisis*. New York: Atheneum, 1969.

Axelrod, Sylvia, et al. "Hospitalized Offspring of Holocaust Survivors." *Bulletin of the Menninger Clinic* 44 (1980): 1–14.

Bankier, David. *The Germans and the Final Solution: Public Opinion under Nazism*. Oxford: Blackwell, 1992.

Bar-On, Dan. *Legacy of Silence: Encounters with Children of the Third Reich*. Cambridge, MA: Harvard University Press, 1989.

———. *The Indescribable and the Undiscussable: Reconstructing Human Discourse after Trauma*. Budapest: Central European University Press, 1999.

Bartlett, Frederic C. *Remembering: A Study in Experimental and Social Psychology*. Cambridge: Cambridge University Press, 1932.

Bauder, David. "For TV Networks, Big Coverage Day." *Associated Press Online*, January 19, 1999.

Bauman, Zygmunt. *Modernity and the Holocaust*. Expanded edition. Ithaca, NY: Cornell University Press, 2000 [1989].

Baumgartner, Mary P. *The Moral Order of a Suburb*. New York: Oxford University Press, 1988.

Beamish, Thomas D. "Accumulating Trouble: Complex Organization, A Culture of Silence, and A Secret Spill." *Social Problems* 47 (2000): 473–98.

———. *Silent Spill: The Organization of an Industrial Crisis*. Cambridge, MA: MIT Press, 2002.

Billig, Michael. *Freudian Repression: Conversation Creating the Unconscious*. Cambridge: Cambridge University Press, 1999.

Bird, Frederick B. *The Muted Conscience: Moral Silence and the Practice of Ethics in Business*. Westport, CT: Quorum Books, 1996.

Bloch, Donald A. "Foreword." In *No Reason To Talk About It: Families Confront the Nuclear Taboo*, by David S. Greenwald and Steven J. Zeitlin, vii–x. New York: W. W. Norton, 1987.

Bok, Sissela. *Secrets: On the Ethics of Concealment and Revelation*. New York: Vintage Books, 1989 [1983].

Bosk, Charles L. *Forgive and Remember: Managing Medical Failure*. Chicago: University of Chicago Press, 1979.

Boston Women's Health Book Collective. *Our Bodies, Ourselves: A Book by and for Women*. New York: Simon and Schuster, 1973.

Bouvard, Marguerite G. *Revolutionizing Motherhood: The Mothers of the Plaza de Mayo*. Wilmington, DE: Scholarly Resources Inc., 1994.

Brasch, Rudolph. *How Did It Begin? Customs and Superstitions and Their Romantic Origins*. Croydon, Australia: Longmans, Green & Co., 1965.

Brekhus, Wayne. "Social Marking and the Mental Coloring of Identity: Sexual Identity Construction and Maintenance in the United States." *Sociological Forum* 11 (1996): 497–522.

———. "A Sociology of the Unmarked: Redirecting Our Focus." *Sociological Theory* 16 (1998): 34–51.

Breznitz, Shlomo (ed.). *The Denial of Stress*. New York: International Universities Press, 1983.

Brison, Susan J. *Aftermath: Violence and the Remaking of a Self*. Princeton, NJ: Princeton University Press, 2002.

Brown, Penelope, and Stephen C. Levinson. *Politeness: Some Universals in Language Use*. Cambridge: Cambridge University Press, 1987 [1978].

Brown, Stephanie. *Treating Adult Children of Alcoholics: A Developmental Perspective*. New York: John Wiley, 1988.

Bruneau, Thomas J. "Communicative Silences: Forms and Functions." *Journal of Communication* 23 (1973): 17–46.

Bumiller, Elisabeth, and Patrick E. Tyler. "Putin Questions U.S. Terror Allies." *New York Times*, November 23, 2002, A1, A10.

Butler, Sandra. *Conspiracy of Silence: The Trauma of Incest*. San Francisco: Volcano Press, 1985.

Casciani, Dominic. "How the Media Covered Up the Scandal." *BBC News* (World Edition), January 30, 2003. http://news.bbc.co.uk/2/hi/uk_news/2707571.stm

Caute, David. *The Espionage of the Saints: Two Essays on Silence and the State*. London: Hamish Hamilton, 1986.

"Cheney's Daughter a Flash Point." *CBS News* (online edition), October 15, 2004. www.cbsnews.com/stories/2004/10/15/politics/main649514.shtml

Cheung, King-Kok. *Articulate Silences: Hisaye Yamamoto, Maxine Hong Kingston, Joy Kogawa*. Ithaca, NY: Cornell University Press, 1993.

Chuck 45. "An Elephant in their Midst." October 9, 2000. www.thegully.com/essays/gaymundo/001009elephant.html

Cialdini, Robert B. *Influence: Science and Practice*. Third Edition. New York: HarperCollins, 1993.

Clemetson, Lynette. "Proposed Marriage Ban Splits Washington's Gays." *New York Times*, July 25, 2004, A17.

"Clinton's 'Hunker-Down' Strategy Holds: President Sidesteps Most Things Lewinsky at Press Conference with U.K.'s Blair." www.cnn.com/ALLPOLITICS/1998/02/06/clinton.blair.presser

Cohen, Bernard C. *The Press and Foreign Policy*. Princeton: Princeton University Press, 1963.

Cohen, Stanley. *States of Denial: Knowing about Atrocities and Suffering*. Cambridge: Polity, 2001.

Cohen, Tamar. "Incest: On Keeping the Secret." In *Knowing and Remaining Silent: Mechanisms of Silencing and Denial in*

Israeli Society [in Hebrew], ed. Hanna Herzog and Kineret Lahad. Jerusalem: Van Leer Institute, forthcoming.

Comte, Auguste. *Cours de Philosophie Positive.* In *Auguste Comte and Positivism: The Essential Writings*, ed. Gertrud Lenzer, 71–306. New York: Harper Torchbooks, 1975 [1830–42].

Conroy, Pat. *The Prince of Tides.* New York: Bantam, 2002 [1986].

Cozzens, Donald. *Sacred Silence: Denial and the Crisis in the Church.* Collegeville, MN: The Liturgical Press, 2002.

Crossen, Cynthia. "Know Thy Father." *Wall Street Journal*, March 4, 1997, A16.

Dauenhauer, Bernard P. *Silence: The Phenomenon and Its Ontological Significance.* Bloomington: Indiana University Press, 1980.

Davidson, Shamai. "The Clinical Effects of Massive Psychic Trauma in Families of Holocaust Survivors." *Journal of Marital and Family Therapy* 6 (1980): 11–21.

Davis, Murray S. *Smut: Erotic Reality / Obscene Ideology.* Chicago: University of Chicago Press, 1983.

DeGloma, Thomas E. "Memory and the Cognitive Masking of Child Sex Abuse: Framing and Cognitive Asymmetries of Power in the Family." Paper presented at the annual meeting of the American Sociological Association, Atlanta, August 2003.

———. "'Safe Space' and Contested Memories: Survivor Movements and the Foundation of Alternative Mnemonic Traditions." Paper presented at the "Spaces of Memory, Spaces of Violence" conference, New School University, New York, April 2004.

Dogan, Mattei, and Robert Pahre. *Creative Marginality: Innovation at the Intersections of the Social Sciences.* Boulder, CO: Westview, 1990.

Dowd, Maureen. "Yo, Ayatollahs!" *New York Times*, May 25, 2003, Section 4, 9.

Downs, Anthony. "Up and Down with Ecology: The 'Issue-Attention Cycle.'" *The Public Interest* 28 (1972): 38–50.

Dubner, Stephen J. "Steven the Good." *New York Times*, February 14, 1999, Section 6, 38.

Durkheim, Emile. *The Elementary Forms of Religious Life*. New York: Free Press, 1995 [1912].

Earle, Alice M. *Curious Punishments of Bygone Days*. Chicago: Herbert F. Stone & Co., 1896.

Eliasoph, Nina. *Avoiding Politics: How Americans Produce Apathy in Everyday Life*. Cambridge: Cambridge University Press, 1998.

Emerson, Joan P. "Behavior in Private Places: Sustaining Definitions of Reality in Gynecological Examinations." In *Recent Sociology No. 2: Patterns of Communicative Behavior*, ed. Hans-Peter Dreitzel, 74–93. London: Macmillan, 1970.

"Ending Legal Secrecy." *New York Times*, September 5, 2002, A22.

Entine, Jon. *Taboo: Why Black Athletes Dominate Sports and Why We're Afraid To Talk about It*. New York: PublicAffairs, 2000.

Farberow, Norman L. "Introduction." In *Taboo Topics*, 1–7. New York: Atheling Books, 1966 [1963].

Farley, Christopher J. "What Bill Cosby Should Be Talking About." *Time* (online edition), June 3, 2004. www.time.com/time/nation/article/0,8599,645801,00.html

Farragher, Thomas. "Church Cloaked in Culture of Silence." *Boston Globe*, February 24, 2002. www.pulitzer.org/year/2003/public-service/works/globe9.html

Farrey, Tom. "Defining Bravery in College Sports." October 7, 2003. http://espn.go.com/ncaa/s/2003/1006/1632030.html#pop3

Faulkner, Peter. "Exposing Risks of Nuclear Disaster." In *Whistle Blowing: Loyalty and Dissent in the Corporation*, ed. Alan F. Westin, 39–54. New York: McGraw-Hill, 1981.

Felman, Shoshana, and Dori Laub (eds.). *Testimony: Crises of Witnessing in Literature, Psychoanalysis, and History*. New York: Routledge, 1992.

Fingarette, Herbert. *Self-Deception*. London: Routledge & Kegan Paul, 1969.

Fishman, Mark. "Crime Waves as Ideology." *Social Problems* 25 (1978): 531–43.

Fleck, Ludwik. *Genesis and Development of a Scientific Fact*. Chicago: University of Chicago Press, 1981 [1935].

Flesch, Rudolf. *The New Book of Unusual Quotations*. New York: Harper and Row, 1966.

Foster, Johanna. "Condom Negotiation and the Politics of Relevance." Unpublished manuscript, Rutgers University, Department of Sociology, 1995.

Foucault, Michel. *The History of Sexuality*, vol. 1. New York: Pantheon, 1978 [1976].

Frank, Leonard R. (ed.). *Random House Webster's Quotationary*. New York: Random House, 1998.

Fraser, Sylvia. *My Father's House: A Memoir of Incest and of Healing*. New York: Perennial Library, 1989 [1987].

Fremont, Helen. *After Long Silence: A Memoir*. New York: Delta Books, 1999.

Fresco, Nadine. "Remembering the Unknown." *International Review of Psycho-Analysis* 11 (1984): 417–27. [Originally published in 1981.]

Freud, Sigmund. *The Psychopathology of Everyday Life*. New York: W. W. Norton, 1960 [1901].

Freyd, Jennifer J. *Betrayal Trauma: The Logic of Forgetting Childhood Abuse*. Cambridge, MA: Harvard University Press, 1996.

Friedan, Betty. *The Feminine Mystique*. New York: W. W. Norton, 1963.

Friedman, Asia. "Sex Seen: The Socio-Optical Construction of Sexed Bodies." Paper presented at the annual meeting of the American Sociological Association, San Francisco, August 2004.

Gadamer, Hans-Georg. *Truth and Method*. New York: Crossroad, 1975 [1960].

Gans, Herbert J. *Deciding What's News: A Study of CBS Evening News, NBC Nightly News, Newsweek, and Time.* New York: Random House, 1979.

Garfinkel, Harold. "Studies of the Routine Grounds of Everyday Activities." In *Studies in Ethnomethodology*, 35–75. Englewood Cliffs, NJ: Prentice-Hall, 1967 [1964].

Gawande, Atul. *Complications: A Surgeon's Notes on an Imperfect Science.* New York: Picador, 2002.

Germana, Rachelle. "Domestic Violence: A Cognitive Approach." Unpublished paper, Rutgers University, Department of Sociology, 2002.

Gettleman, Jeffrey. "Thurmond Family Struggles with Difficult Truth." *New York Times*, December 20, 2003, A1, A13.

Geuss, Raymond. *Public Goods, Private Goods.* Princeton, NJ: Princeton University Press, 2001.

Gladwell, Malcolm. *The Tipping Point: How Little Things Can Make a Big Difference.* New York: Little, Brown, and Co., 2000.

Glaser, Barney G., and Anselm L. Strauss. *Awareness of Dying.* Chicago: University of Chicago Press, 1965.

Glazer, Myron P., and Penina M. Glazer. *The Whistleblowers: Exposing Corruption in Government and Industry.* New York: Basic Books, 1989.

Goffman, Erving. "On Face Work: An Analysis of Ritual Elements in Social Interaction." In *Interaction Ritual: Essays on Face-to-Face Behavior*, 5–45. Garden City, NY: Doubleday Anchor, 1967 [1955].

———. "Embarrassment and Social Organization." *American Journal of Sociology* 62 (1956): 264–74.

——— *The Presentation of Self in Everyday Life*. Garden City, NY: Doubleday Anchor, 1959.

———. "Fun in Games." In *Encounters: Two Studies in the Sociology of Interaction*, 17–81. Indianapolis: Bobbs-Merrill, 1961.

———. *Behavior in Public Places: Notes on the Social Organization of Gatherings.* New York: Free Press, 1963.

———. *Frame Analysis: An Essay on the Organization of Experience.* New York: Harper Colophon, 1974.

———. "Footing." In *Forms of Talk*, 124–59. Philadelphia: University of Pennsylvania Press, 1981 [1979].

Goldsmith, Martin. *The Inextinguishable Symphony: A True Story of Music and Love in Nazi Germany.* New York: John Wiley & Sons, 2000.

Goleman, Daniel. *Vital Lies, Simple Truths: The Psychology of Self-Deception.* New York: Touchstone Books, 1986.

Goode, Erich, and Nachman Ben-Yehuda. *Moral Panics: The Social Construction of Deviance.* Oxford: Blackwell, 1994.

Goodstein, Laurie. "Lawyer for Church Says He Hid His Own Sexual Abuse by Priest." *New York Times*, November 25, 2003, A1, A18.

Graziano, Frank. *Divine Violence: Spectacle, Psychosexuality, and Radical Christianity in the Argentine "Dirty War."* Boulder, CO: Westview, 1992.

Greenwald, David S., and Steven J. Zeitlin. *No Reason To Talk about It: Families Confront the Nuclear Taboo.* New York: W. W. Norton, 1987.

Griffin, Susan. *A Chorus of Stones: The Private Life of War.* New York: Doubleday, 1992.

Gross, John. "Intimations of Mortality." In *Fair of Speech: The Uses of Euphemism*, ed. D. J. Enright, 203–19. Oxford: Oxford University Press, 1985.

Gross, Larry. *Contested Closets: The Politics and Ethics of Outing.* Minneapolis: University of Minnesota Press, 1993.

Gurevitch, Zali. "Dialectical Dialogue: The Struggle for Speech, Repressive Silence, and the Shift to Multiplicity." *British Journal of Sociology* 52 (2001): 87–104.

Haidu, Peter. "The Dialectics of Unspeakability: Language, Silence, and the Narratives of Desubjectification." In *Probing the Limits of Representation: Nazism and the "Final Solution,"* ed. Saul Friedlander, 277–99. Cambridge, MA: Harvard University Press, 1992.

Hall, Edward T. *The Hidden Dimension*. Garden City, NY: Doubleday, 1966.

Hammarskjöld, Dag. *Markings*. New York: Alfred A. Knopf, 1964 [1963].

Harper, Jennifer. "Media Highlights Surreal Day with Trial, State of the Union." *Washington Times*, January 19, 1999, A11.

Harrison, Kathryn. *Thicker than Water*. New York: Random House, 1991.

———. *The Kiss*. New York: Avon Books, 1997.

Hays, Kate F. "The Conspiracy of Silence Revisited: Group Therapy with Adult Survivors of Incest." *Journal of Group Psychotherapy, Psychodrama, and Sociometry* 39 (1987): 143–56.

Herman, Judith L. *Father-Daughter Incest*. Cambridge, MA: Harvard University Press, 1981.

———. "Foreword." In *Conspiracy of Silence: The Trauma of Incest*, by Sandra Butler, ix. San Francisco: Volcano Press, 1985.

———. *Trauma and Recovery*. New York: Basic Books, 1992.

Hilberg, Raul. *Perpetrators, Victims, Bystanders: The Jewish Catastrophe 1933–1945*. New York: HarperCollins, 1992.

Hillenbrandt, Fritz K. M. *Underground Humour in Nazi Germany 1933–1945*. London: Routledge, 1995.

Hochhuth, Rolf. *The Deputy*. New York: Grove Press, 1964 [1963].

Hochschild, Arlie. *The Managed Heart: Commercialization of Human Feeling*. Berkeley: University of California Press, 1983.

Horwitz, Gordon J. *In the Shadow of Death: Living Outside the Gates of Mauthausen*. New York: Free Press, 1990.

Hotchkiss, John. "Children and Conduct in a Ladino Community in Chiapas, Mexico." *American Anthropologist* 69 (1967): 711–18.

Hudson, Audrey. "Biologists' Roles in Lynx-Hair Fraud under Review." *Washington Times*, April 23, 2002.

Hughes, Everett C. "Good People and Dirty Work." In *The Sociological Eye: Selected Papers*, 87–97. Chicago: Aldine, 1971 [1962].

Hulme, Kathryn. *The Nun's Story*. Boston: Little, Brown & Co., 1956.

Ibsen, Henrik. "An Enemy of the People." In *Six Plays by Henrik Ibsen*, trans. Eva Le Gallienne, 157–255. New York: The Modern Library, 1957 [1882].

Jasper, James M. *The Art of Moral Protest: Culture, Biography, and Creativity in Social Movements*. Chicago: University of Chicago Press, 1997.

Jaworski, Adam. *The Power of Silence: Social and Pragmatic Perspectives*. Newbury Park, CA: Sage, 1993.

Jensen, Derrick. *A Language Older Than Words*. New York: Context Books, 2000.

Johansson, Warren, and William A. Percy. *Outing: Shattering the Conspiracy of Silence*. Binghamton, NY: Haworth Press, 1994.

Johnson, Vernon E. *I'll Quit Tomorrow*. New York: Harper and Row, 1973.

————. *Intervention: How To Help Someone Who Doesn't Want Help*. Minneapolis, MN: Johnson Institute Books, 1986.

Jordan, Mark. *The Silence of Sodom: Homosexuality in Modern Catholicism*. Chicago: University of Chicago Press, 2000.

Juan Manuel, Don. "What Happened to the King and the Tricksters Who Made Cloth." In *The Book of Count Lucanor and Patronio*, trans. John E. Keller and L. Clark Keating, 130–33. Lexington: University Press of Kentucky, 1977 [1335].

Katriel, Tamar. *Talking Straight: Dugri Speech in Israeli Sabra Culture*. Cambridge: Cambridge University Press, 1986.

Katz, Jay. *The Silent World of Doctor and Patient*. New York: Free Press, 1984.

Kern, Stephen. *The Culture of Time and Space 1880–1918*. Cambridge, MA: Harvard University Press, 1983.

Klietsch, Ronald G. "Clothesline Patterns and Covert Behavior." *Journal of Marriage and the Family* 27 (1965): 78–80.

Klinenberg, Eric. *Heat Wave: A Social Autopsy of Disaster in Chicago*. Chicago: University of Chicago Press, 2002.

Koestler, Arthur. *The Act of Creation*. New York: Macmillan, 1964.

Kristof, Nicholas D. "Are the Saudis the Enemy?" *New York Times*, October 22, 2002, A31.

Krugman, Paul. "Gotta Have Faith." *New York Times*, December 17, 2002, A35.

Kuhn, Thomas S. *The Structure of Scientific Revolutions*. Chicago: University of Chicago Press, 1962.

Kuran, Timur. *Private Truths, Public Lies: The Social Consequences of Preference Falsification*. Cambridge, MA: Harvard University Press, 1995.

Kwiatkowska, Alina. "Silence across Modalities." In *Silence: Interdisciplinary Perspectives*, ed. Adam Jaworski, 329–37. Berlin and New York: Mouton de Gruyter, 1997.

Laing, Ronald D. "The Politics of the Family." In *The Politics of the Family and Other Essays*, 65–124. New York: Pantheon Books, 1971 [1969].

Lanzmann, Claude. *Shoah: An Oral History of the Holocaust*. New York: Pantheon, 1985.

Laor, Yitzhak. "We Write You, Homeland." In *Narratives with No Natives: Essays on Israeli Literature* [in Hebrew], 115–70. Tel Aviv: Hotzaat Hakibbutz Hameuchad, 1995.

Laqueur, Walter. *The Terrible Secret: Suppression of the Truth about Hitler's "Final Solution."* Boston: Little, Brown & Co., 1980.

Latané, Bibb, and John M. Darley. *The Unresponsive Bystander: Why Doesn't He Help?* New York: Appleton-Century-Crofts, 1970.

Lev, Eleonora. "Lolita: Her Real Story" [in Hebrew]. *Ha'aretz Literary Supplement*, October 7, 1998, 5.

Lewis, Jan E. "The White Jeffersons." In *Sally Hemings and Thomas Jefferson: History, Memory, and Civic Culture*, ed. Jan E. Lewis and Peter S. Onuf, 127–60. Charlottesville: University Press of Virginia, 1999.

Lewis, Jan E., and Peter S. Onuf (eds.). *Sally Hemings and Thomas Jefferson: History, Memory, and Civic Culture*. Charlottesville: University Press of Virginia, 1999.

Lifton, Robert J. "Imagining the Real." In *Indefensible Weapons: The Political and Psychological Case against Nuclearism*, eds. Robert J. Lifton and Richard Falk, 3–125. New York: Basic Books, 1982.

———. *The Nazi Doctors: Medical Killing and the Psychology of Genocide*. New York: Basic Books, 1986.

Lifton, Robert J., and Greg Mitchell. *Hiroshima in America: Fifty Years of Denial*. New York: G. P. Putnam's Sons, 1995.

Liptak, Adam. "South Carolina Judges Voted to Ban Secret Court Settlements." *New York Times*, September 2, 2002, A1.

Lister, Eric D. "Forced Silence: A Neglected Dimension of Trauma." *American Journal of Psychiatry* 139 (1982): 872–76.

Luchterhand, Elmer. "Knowing and Not Knowing: Involvement in Nazi Genocide." In *Our Common History: The Transformation of Europe*, ed. Paul Thompson, 251–72. Atlantic Highlands, NJ: Humanities Press, 1982.

Machotka, Pavel, et al. "Incest as a Family Affair." *Family Process* 6 (1967): 98–116.

Mack, Arien, and Irvin Rock. *Inattentional Blindness*. Cambridge, MA: MIT Press, 1998.

Makiya, Kanan. *Cruelty and Silence: War, Tyranny, Uprising, and the Arab World*. New York: W. W. Norton, 1993.

Maloff, Chalda, and Susan M. Wood. *Business and Social Etiquette with Disabled People: A Guide to Getting Along with Persons Who*

Have Impairments of Mobility, Vision, Hearing, or Speech. Springfield, IL: Charles C. Thomas, 1988.

Manji, Irshad. *The Trouble with Islam: A Muslim's Call for Reform in Her Faith.* Toronto: Random House of Canada, 2003.

Mann, Thomas. *The Magic Mountain.* New York: Vintage Books, 1969 [1924].

Martin, Judith. *Miss Manners' Guide for the Turn-of-the-Millennium.* New York: Fireside, 1990.

Martin, Patricia Y., and Robert A. Hummer. "Fraternities and Rape on Campus." *Gender and Society* 3 (1989): 457–73.

Masson, Jeffrey M. *The Assault on Truth: Freud's Suppression of the Seduction Theory.* New York: Farrar, Straus and Giroux, 1984.

McCombs, Maxwell E., and Donald L. Shaw. "The Agenda-Setting Function of Mass Media." *Public Opinion Quarterly* 36 (1972): 176–87.

Meyrowitz, Joshua, "The Press Rejects a Candidate." *Columbia Journalism Review*, March/April 1992, 46–47.

Miceli, Marcia P., and Janet P. Near. *Blowing the Whistle: The Organizational and Legal Implications for Companies and Employees.* New York: Lexington, 1992.

Mieder, Wolfgang. "The Proverbial Three Wise Monkeys." *Midwestern Journal of Language and Folklore* 7 (1981): 5–38.

———. *Tradition and Innovation in Folk Literature.* Hanover, NH: University Press of New England, 1987.

Miethe, Terence D. *Whistleblowing at Work: Tough Choices in Exposing Fraud, Waste, and Abuse on the Job.* Boulder, CO: Westview, 1999.

Milgram, Stanley. *Obedience to Authority: An Experimental View.* New York: Harper and Row, 1974.

Miller, Jonathan. *The Body in Question.* New York: Random House, 1978.

Milliken, Frances J., et al. "An Exploratory Study of Employee Silence: Issues that Employees Don't Communicate Upward and Why." *Journal of Management Studies* 40 (2003): 1453–76.

Mills, Alice, and Jeremy Smith. "Introduction." In *Utter Silence: Voicing the Unspeakable*, 1–15. New York: Peter Lang, 2001.

Mills, C. Wright. *The Sociological Imagination*. London: Oxford University Press, 1959.

Mitscherlich, Alexander, and Margarete Mitscherlich. *The Inability to Mourn: Principles of Collective Behavior*. New York: Grove Press, 1975 [1967].

"Moore Fires Oscar Anti-War Salvo." March 24, 2003. http://news.bbc.co.uk/1/hi/entertainment/film/2879857.stm

Moore, Michael. "A Letter to George W. Bush on the Eve of War." *AlterNet.Org*, March 17, 2003. http://72.14.207.104/search?q=cache:T-1hmuwkCmUJ:www.alternet.org/story.html%3FStoryID%3D15406+%22A+Letter+to+George+W.+Bush+on+the+Eve+of+War%22&hl=en

Morris, Benny. *The Birth of the Palestinian Refugee Problem, 1947–1949*. New York: Cambridge University Press, 1987.

Morrison, Elizabeth W., and Frances J. Milliken. "Organizational Silence: A Barrier to Change and Development in a Pluralistic World." *Academy of Management Review* 25 (2000): 706–25.

Moscovici, Serge. "Social Influence and Conformity." In vol. 2 of *Handbook of Social Psychology*, ed. Gardner Lindzey and Elliot Aronson, 347–412. Third Edition. New York: Random House, 1985.

"Mrs. Simpson Had Secret Lover." CNN.com, January 30, 2003. www.cnn.com/2003/WORLD/europe/01/29/edward.files/

Mullaney, Jamie L. "Like A Virgin: Temptation, Resistance, and the Construction of Identities Based on 'Not Doings.'" *Qualitative Sociology* 24 (2001): 3–24.

———. *Everyone Is NOT Doing It: Abstinence and Personal Identity*. Chicago: University of Chicago Press, 2005.

Nason-Clark, Nancy. "Has the Silence Been Shattered or Does a Holy Hush Still Prevail?: Defining Violence against Women within Christian Churches." In *Bad Pastors: Clergy Misconduct in Modern America*, ed. Anson Shupe et al., 69–89. New York: New York University Press, 2000.

Naveh, Hannah. "The Marital bed." In *Knowing and Remaining Silent: Mechanisms of Silencing and Denial in Israeli Society* [in Hebrew], ed. Hanna Herzog and Kineret Lahad. Jerusalem: Van Leer Institute, forthcoming.

Norgaard, Kari M. "Denial, Privilege and Global Environmental Justice: The Case of Climate Change." Paper presented at the annual meeting of the American Sociological Association, Atlanta, August 2003.

———. "People Want To Protect Themselves A Little Bit: Emotions, Denial and Social Movement Non-Participation—The Case of Global Climate Change." Paper presented at the annual meeting of the American Sociological Association, Atlanta, August 2003.

Office of the Independent Counsel, The. "Referral to the United States House of Representatives Pursuant to Title 28, United States Code, § 595(C)," *New York Times*, September 12, 1998, B1–B16. [Also known as "The Starr Report."]

Orwell, George. *Nineteen Eighty-Four.* New York: New American Library, 1961 [1949].

Perry, Helen S. "Selective Inattention as an Explanatory Concept for U.S. Public Attitudes toward the Atomic Bomb." *Psychiatry* 17 (1954): 225–42.

Peters, Mike. *The Nixon Chronicles.* Dayton, OH: Lorenz Press, 1976.

Petersen, Betsy. *Dancing with Daddy: A Childhood Lost and a Life Regained.* New York: Bantam, 1991.

Pincus, Lily, and Christopher Dare. *Secrets in the Family.* New York: Pantheon Books, 1978.

Pinder, Craig C., and Karen P. Harlos. "Employee Silence: Quiescence and Acquiescence as Responses to Perceived

Injustice." *Research in Personnel and Human Resources Management* 20 (2001): 331–69.

Pinsker, Sanford. "Art as Excess: The 'Voices' of Charlie Parker and Philip Roth." *Partisan Review* 69 (2002): 58–66.

Pirandello, Luigi. *Tonight We Improvise.* New York: Samuel French, 1960 [1932].

Pittenger, Robert E., et al. *The First Five Minutes: A Sample of Microscopic Interview Analysis.* Ithaca, NY: Paul Martineau, 1960.

Pletch, Dan. "Weapons of Mass Distraction: President Bush Wouldn't Want to Talk about the Many Issues which the Iraq Crisis Is Obscuring." *Observer Worldview*, September 29, 2002. www.observer.co.uk/worldview/story/0,11581, 800486,00.html

Pollock, Mica. *Colormute: Race Talk Dilemmas in an American School.* Princeton, NJ: Princeton University Press, 2004.

Pound, Louise. "American Euphemisms for Dying, Death, and Burial." *American Speech* 11 (1936): 195–202.

"President Bill Clinton, Prime Minister Tony Blair Joint News Conference—Feb. 6, 1998." www.cnn.com/ALL POLITICS/1998/02/06/transcripts/clinton

Purcell, Kristen. "In a League of Their Own: Mental Leveling and the Creation of Social Comparability in Sport." *Sociological Forum* 11 (1996): 435–56.

Raine, Nancy V. *After Silence: Rape and My Journey Back.* New York: Crown, 1998.

Redding, W. Charles. "Rocking Boats, Blowing Whistles, and Teaching Speech Communication." *Communication Education* 34 (1985): 245–58.

Robinson, Walter V. "Scores of Priests Involved in Sex Abuse Cases: Settlements Kept Scope of Issue Out of Public Eye." *Boston Globe*, January 31, 2002. www.pulitzer.org/year/2003/ public-service/works/globe5.html

Roche, Helena. *The Addiction Process: From Enabling to Intervention.* Deerfield Beach, FL: Health Communications, 1990.

Rogoff, Barbara. *Apprenticeship in Thinking: Cognitive Development in Social Context.* New York: Oxford University Press, 1990.

Rothschild, Joyce, and Terance D. Miethe. "Whistle-Blower Disclosures and Management Retaliation: The Battle to Control Information about Organization Corruption." *Work and Occupations* 26 (1999): 107–28.

Ryan, Dan. "Getting the Word Out: Notes on the Social Organization of Notification." *Sociological Theory,* forthcoming.

Ryan, Joan. "Guns in Society: The Real Problem." *San Francisco Chronicle,* August 22, 1999, 1, Z1.

Ryan, Kathleen D., and Daniel K. Oestreich. *Driving Fear Out of the Office: How To Overcome the Invisible Barriers to Quality, Productivity, and Innovation.* San Francisco: Jossey-Bass, 1991.

Samarin, William J. "Language of Silence." *Practical Anthropology* 12 (1965): 115–19.

Sanger, David E. "Lewinsky Was Familiar Face to Agents near Clinton's Door." *New York Times,* September 13, 1998, National Section, 35.

Schachtel, Ernest G. *Metamorphosis: On the Development of Affect, Perception, Attention, and Memory.* New York: Basic Books, 1959.

Schlant, Ernestine. *The Language of Silence: West German Literature and the Holocaust.* New York: Routledge, 1999.

Schwartz, Barry. "Vengeance and Forgiveness: The Uses of Beneficence in Social Control." *School Review* 86 (1978): 655–68.

Sciolino, Elaine, and Neil MacFarquhar. "Naming of Hijackers as Saudis May Further Erode Ties to U.S." *New York Times,* October 25, 2001, A1, B4.

Segil, Larraine. *Dynamic Leader, Adaptive Organization: Ten Essential Traits for Managers.* New York: John Wiley & Sons, 2002.

Sherif, Muzafer, and Carolyn W. Sherif. *Social Psychology.* New York: Harper and Row, 1969.

Sheriff, Robin E. "Exposing Silence as Cultural Censorship: A Brazilian Case." *American Anthropologist* 102 (2000): 114–32.

Shilts, Randy. *And the Band Played On: Politics, People, and the AIDS Epidemic*. New York: St. Martin's Press, 1987.

Simmel, Georg. "Quantitative Aspects of the Group." In *The Sociology of Georg Simmel*, ed. Kurt H. Wolff, 87–177. New York: Free Press, 1950 [1908].

———. "The Secret and the Secret Society." In *The Sociology of Georg Simmel*, ed. Kurt H. Wolff, 307–76. New York: Free Press, 1950 [1908].

———. "The Field of Sociology." In *The Sociology of Georg Simmel*, ed. Kurt H. Wolff, 3–25. New York: Free Press, 1950 [1917].

Simpson, Ruth. "The Germ Culture." Paper presented at the annual meeting of the American Sociological Association, Chicago, 2002.

Smiley, Jane. *A Thousand Acres*. New York: Fawcett Columbine, 1991.

Sobkowiak, Włodzimierz. "Silence and Markedness Theory." In *Silence: Interdisciplinary Perspectives*, ed. Adam Jaworski, 39–61. Berlin and New York: Mouton de Gruyter, 1997.

Solzhenitsyn, Aleksandr. *One Day in the Life of Ivan Denisovich*. New York: Praeger, 1963 [1962].

Sprague, Jo, and Gary L. Ruud. "Boat Rocking in the High-Technology Culture." *American Behavioral Scientist* 32 (1988): 169–93.

Staton, Jana, et al. *A Few Months to Live: Different Paths to Life's End*. Washington, DC: Georgetown University Press, 2001.

Stein, Arlene. "Trauma Stories, Identity Work, and the Politics of Recognition." In *De-ghettoizing the Holocaust: Collective Memory, Identity, and Trauma*, ed. Judith M. Gerson and Diane L. Wolf. Durham, NC: Duke University Press, forthcoming.

Steiner, John. "Turning a Blind Eye: The Cover Up for Oedipus." *International Review of Psycho-Analysis* 12 (1985): 161–72.

————. "The Retreat from Truth to Omnipotence in Sophocles' Oedipus at Colonus." *International Review of Psycho-Analysis* 17 (1990): 227–37.

————. *Psychic Retreats: Pathological Organisations in Psychotic, Neurotic, and Borderline Patients.* London: Routledge, 1993.

Stinchcombe, Arthur L. *Constructing Social Theories.* New York: Harcourt, Brace & World, 1968.

Stohl, Michael. "Outside of a Small Circle of Friends: States, Genocide, Mass Killing and the Role of Bystanders." *Journal of Peace Research* 24 (1987): 151–66.

Stone, Christopher D. *Should Trees Have Standing?* Los Altos, CA: William Kaufmann, 1974.

Stone, I. F. "It Pays To Be Ignorant." *New York Review of Books,* August 9, 1973, 6–9.

Stuart, Elizabeth. *Chosen: Gay Catholic Priests Tell Their Stories.* London: Geoffrey Chapman, 1993.

Swarns, Rachel L. "Mugabe's Aides Declare Him Winner of Zimbabwe Vote." *New York Times,* March 14, 2002, A3.

Tannen, Deborah. "Silence as Conflict Management in Fiction and Drama: Pinter's *Betrayal* and a Short Story, 'Great Wits.'" In *Conflict Talk: Sociolinguistic Investigations of Arguments in Conversations,* ed. Allen D. Grimshaw, 260–79. Cambridge: Cambridge University Press, 1990.

Tannen, Deborah, and Muriel Saville-Troike (eds.). *Perspectives on Silence.* Norwood, NJ: Ablex, 1985.

Taussig, Michael. *Defacement: Public Secrecy and the Labor of the Negative.* Stanford: Stanford University Press, 1999.

Taylor, Jill M., et al. *Between Voice and Silence: Women and Girls, Race and Relationship.* Cambridge, MA: Harvard University Press, 1995.

Tiersma, Peter. "The Language of Silence." *Rutgers Law Review* 48 (1995): 1–99.

Timerman, Jacobo. *Prisoner Without a Name, Cell Without a Number*. New York: Alfred A. Knopf, 1981.

Tolczyk, Dariusz. *See No Evil: Literary Cover-Ups and Discoveries of the Soviet Camp Experience*. New Haven, CT: Yale University Press, 1999.

Truffaut, François. *Hitchcock*. Revised Edition. New York: Touchstone, 1985 [1983].

Typpo, Marion H., and Jill M. Hastings. *An Elephant in the Living Room: A Leader's Guide for Helping Children of Alcoholics*. Center City, MN: Hazelden, 1984.

Van Dyne, Linn, et al. "Conceptualizing Employee Silence and Employee Voice as Multidimensional Constructs." *Journal of Management Studies* 40 (2003): 1359–92.

Vaughan, Diane. *Uncoupling: Turning Points in Intimate Relationships*. New York: Oxford University Press, 1986.

Vellacott, Philip. *Sophocles and Oedipus: A Study of Oedipus Tyrannus with a New Translation*. Ann Arbor: University of Michigan Press, 1971.

Volkan, Vamik D., et al. *The Third Reich in the Unconscious: Transgenerational Transmission and Its Consequences*. New York: Brunner-Routledge, 2002.

Wagner, Jill. "Arab Talk Radio Host Seeks To Break Taboos." *MSNBC News* (online edition), July 22, 2004. http://thejuice. msnbc.com/id/5466283

Wajnryb, Ruth. *The Silence: How Tragedy Shapes Talk*. Crows Nest, Australia: Allen & Unwin, 2001.

Weinberg, Martin S. "Sexual Modesty, Social Meanings, and the Nudist Camp." *Social Problems* 12 (1965): 311–18.

Westin, Alan F. "Introduction." In *Whistle Blowing: Loyalty and Dissent in the Corporation*, ed. Alan F. Westin, 1–15. New York: McGraw-Hill, 1981.

White, Ralph K., et al. "Studies in Adjustment to Visible Injuries: Evaluation of Curiosity by the Injured." *Journal of Abnormal and Social Psychology* 43 (1948): 13–28.

White, Robert K. "Family Intervention: Background, Principles, and Other Strategies." In *Addiction Intervention: Strategies to Motivate Treatment-Seeking Behavior*, ed. Robert K. White and Deborah G. Wright, 7–20. New York: Haworth Press, 1998.

Wiseman, Hadas, et al. "Parental Communication of Holocaust Experiences and Interpersonal Patterns in Offspring of Holocaust Survivors." *International Journal of Behavioral Development* 26 (2002): 371–81.

Wurgaft, Nurit. "She Turns On the Mike and Lifts Up the Rug." *Haaretz*, May 31, 2004. www.haaretz.com/hasen/pages/ShArt.jhtml?itemNo=431602&contrassID=2&subContrassID=20&sbSubContrassID=0&listSrc=Y

Wurmser, Léon. "Blinding the Eye of the Mind: Denial, Impulsive Action, and Split Identity." In *Denial: A Clarification of Concepts and Research*, ed. E. L. Edelstein et al., 175–201. New York: Plenum, 1989.

Zelizer, Barbie. *Remembering to Forget: Holocaust Memory through the Camera's Eye*. Chicago: University of Chicago Press, 1998.

Zerubavel, Eviatar. *Patterns of Time in Hospital Life: A Sociological Perspective*. Chicago: University of Chicago Press, 1979.

———. "If Simmel Were a Fieldworker: On Formal Sociological Theory and Analytical Field Research." *Symbolic Interaction* 3, no. 2 (1980): 25–33.

———. "Personal Information and Social Life." *Symbolic Interaction* 5, no. 1 (1982): 97–109.

———. *The Seven-Day Circle: The History and Meaning of the Week*. Chicago: University of Chicago Press, 1989 [1985].

———. *The Fine Line: Making Distinctions in Everyday Life*. Chicago: University of Chicago Press, 1993 [1991].

———. *Terra Cognita: The Mental Discovery of America*. New Brunswick, NJ: Rutgers University Press, 1992.

———. "The Rigid, the Fuzzy, and the Flexible: Notes on the Mental Sculpting of Academic Identity." *Social Research* 62 (1995): 1093–1106.

————. *Social Mindscapes: An Invitation to Cognitive Sociology*. Cambridge, MA: Harvard University Press, 1997.

————. "The Elephant in the Room: Notes on the Social Organization of Denial." Paper presented at the "Toward a Sociology of Culture and Cognition" conference, Rutgers University, November 1999.

————. "The Elephant in the Room: Notes on the Social Organization of Denial." In *Culture in Mind: Toward a Sociology of Culture and Cognition*, ed. Karen A. Cerulo, 21–27. New York: Routledge, 2002.

————. *Time Maps: Collective Memory and the Social Shape of the Past*. Chicago: University of Chicago Press, 2003.

————. "Generally Speaking: The Logic and Mechanics of Social Pattern Analysis." Paper presented at the annual meeting of the American Sociological Association, San Francisco, August 2004.

Zerubavel, Noam. "Allegorical Recognition of Truth and Identity in *Oedipus Rex*." Unpublished paper, Columbia University, 2003.

Author Index

Subject Index

blind spots, 4
brutality, 6, 8
Bush, George W., 36, 63, 66, 71
Butler, Sandra, 78
"button your lip," 44
bystanders, 6, 55-56

Cage, John, 33
"calling a spade a spade," 67
cartoons, 11-12, 62
Cassandra, 69
Celebration, The, 71
censorship, 39-40
Cheney, Dick, 10, 75
children, 2, 7, 10-11, 20-21, 23-24, 28, 39-40, 45, 49, 52, 75, 80
child sexual abuse, 43, 45, 52, 55, 64, 71, 76, 78, 85
Clinton, Bill, 12-13, 45, 48, 67
closets, 50, 64
co-denial, 47-48, 51
co-ignoring, 3, 84
Colbert, Stephen, 67
collusion, 3, 37, 80, 87
communication: conventions of, 20; open, x, 64, 82, 85; social organization of, 34
communities, 5, 20, 25, 27, 38
concentration camps, 6, 39-41, 50
confidentiality agreements, 42
conspiracies of noise, 52
conspiracies of publicity, 64
conspiracies of silence, 2, 4-6, 8-9, 11, 13-14, 17, 29, 34, 47-49, 51-52, 54-59, 61-63, 65-72, 74-79, 81-87; benefits of, 73-78; breaking, 62-72, 74-77; collaborative nature of, 4, 48-52, 84; maintaining, 69, 77; problems posed by, 79-87

conspirators of silence, 3, 15, 51-53, 58, 61-62, 69, 71, 75, 84; number of, 15, 51, 54-56, 69
control, social, 15, 35-39
corroboration, 1-2, 71, 80
corruption, 27, 57, 78, 85
Cosby, Bill, 76-77
couples, 4, 51, 58
cover-ups, 49, 52, 84
curiosity, 21, 26, 31, 35, 40
cynicism, 81

deafness, 5
death, 6, 51, 57
Debini, Suzan, 66
Degas, Edgar, 33
delusion, 2, 74, 80, 86
denial: collective, 3, 10, 14, 48, 58, 87; mutual, 3-4, 47, 49, 51, 58; politics of, 33-45; social dynamics of, 4, 14, 29, 48, 50, 64; social organization of, x, 16, 55; social structure of, 47-59; sociology of, 3; spiral of, 59; vicious cycle of, 58
destabilization, social, 41
deviance, social, 30
deviants, social, 16, 26, 78
"Dirty War," Argentina's, 41, 68
disappearances, 41
discourse: bounds of acceptable, 9, 28-29, 36, 68; public, 3, 15, 63; scope of, 15, 34, 36, 38
discretion, 40, 45, 48-49, 75
discussability, 15, 67, 84
discussion: x, 3, 6, 13, 15-16, 26, 41, 49, 52, 56-57, 63, 67, 81, 84; open, 16, 54-55, 73, 87
disregard, 18-23, 25, 38, 40, 58
distance, social, 54, 82